W9-CCU-231

Ray & Anne Ortlund

CONFIDENT IN CHRIST

Discover Who You Are As A Believer

Portland, Oregon 97266

Unless otherwise indicated, all Scripture references are from the Holy Bible: New International Version, copyright 1973, 1978, 1984 by the International Bible Society. Used by permission of Zondervan Bible Publishers.

Scripture references marked KJV are from the Holy Bible: King James Version.

Scripture references marked NAS are from the New American Standard Bible, © The Lockman Foundation 1960, 1962, 1963, 1968, 1971, 1972, 1973, 1975, 1977. Used by permission.

Scripture references marked Phillips are from J. B. Phillips: The New Testament in Modern English, revised eiditon. © J. B. Phillips 1958, 1960, 1972. Used by permission of Macmillan Publishing Co., Inc.

Cover design by Bruce DeRoos

CONFIDENT IN CHRIST

Published by Multnomah Press
Portland, Oregon 97266

Multnomah Press is a ministry of Multnomah School of the Bible, 8435 N.E. Glisan Street, Portland, Oregon 97220

Printed in the United States of America

Library of Congress Cataloging-in-Publication Data

Ortlund, Raymond C.
Confident in Christ / Ray and Anne Ortlund.
p. cm.
ISBN 0-88070-316-4
1. Mystical union. I. Ortlund, Anne. II. Title.
BT769.077 1989
248.2—dc19

89-31380
CIP

89 90 91 92 93 94 95 96 97 98 - 10 9 8 7 6 5 4 3 2 1

CONTENTS

Introduction

Walt Whitman once went to a lecture on astronomy. The hall was hot and stuffy, and the speaker droned on about the stars until, restless and bored, Whitman couldn't stand it any longer. "I got up," he said, "and went out of the building and looked up to the stars themselves."

Words can easily detract from what it means to be in Christ. Being in Christ is something that can only be understood from the inside—from assenting to it, applying it, and enjoying it. "It is only the completely surrendered heart which knows what it is to be in Christ in the fullest sense of the term."[1] As you read this book, ask God to give you a spirit of obedience. Be hungry to understand your position in Christ, to begin to live in the light of it, and to enjoy the resulting new intimacy you'll discover with Him.

---

1. William Barclay, *The Mind of St. Paul* (New York: Harper and Row, reprinted in 1975), pp. 121, 122.

PRAYER OF SAINT PATRICK

I establish myself today in:
The power of God to guide me,
The might of God to uphold me,
The wisdom of God to teach me,
The eye of God to watch over me,
The ear of God to hear me,
The word of God to speak to me,
The hand of God to protect me,
The way of God to lie before me,
The shield of God to shelter me,
The hosts of God to defend me.
Christ with me, Christ before me,
Christ behind me, Christ within me,
Christ beneath me, Christ above me,
Christ at my right, Christ at my left,
Christ in breadth, Christ in length,
Christ in height, Christ in the heart
of every man who thinks of me,
Christ in the mouth of every man
who speaks to me,
Christ in the ear of every man
who hears me.

~ 1 ~

You Are My Hiding Place

"You are my hiding place . . ." You've probably sung those words. Believers have been singing them for three thousand years.

David sang them first in Psalm 32. He had committed adultery with Bathsheba, murdered her husband, then covered up his acts before he finally confessed. His days were filled with turmoil and guilt and dread and weakness and distraction from duty.

Soon it grew obvious that Bathsheba was pregnant. The servants eyed David and whispered to each other . . .

Uriah her husband died at too convenient a time. The soldiers eyed David and whispered to each other . . .

During the day David would think of what he had done, and his palms would get clammy. He'd think of it at night, and his heart would race. He'd look at violated Bathsheba, his new possession, and he couldn't write psalms, he couldn't pray.

Then the prophet Nathan did what any good pastor should do. He called on David and faced him with the whole mess—and David broke down and confessed the truth: "I have sinned."

And through the pain, at that moment David knew that the back of his sin was broken. He was at last released, he was cleansed, he was whole again. He could pray and write psalms.

"Blessed is he," wrote David,
"whose transgressions are forgiven . . .
When I kept silent,
my bones wasted away
through my groaning all day long.
For day and night
your hand was heavy upon me;
my strength was sapped
as in the heat of summer.

"Then I acknowledged my sin to you . . .
I said, 'I will confess
my transgressions to the Lord'—
and you forgave
the guilt of my sin."

"Oh," said David to the Lord, with all the fervor of his heart—

"You are my hiding place;
you will protect me . . .
and surround me. . . . "

One way or another, you're a David.

And so are the two of us. We are well acquainted with misery for our sins. We know about being uncomfortable because we've said one thing to one person and something slightly different to another—and they could compare notes.

As a couple we've lost our tempers with each other and said things that hurt for a long time afterward; we've punished one child and discovered another did it; we've been tender when we should have been tough, and tough when we should have been tender.

We know about sins of the mind and sins of self-centeredness and sins of insensitivity to others, and the trauma and confusion it all brings.

So do you. And through the pains in your life, through your embarrassment over your sins, through your insecurities, through the times you botch up your relationships with those around you— don't you need a place to hide, a place to get cleansed and forgiven, a place of comfort, a safe spot where you can withdraw and regroup?

The Christian has such a place: Christ Himself.

"In Christ," "in the Lord," "in Him"—this phrase or its equivalent occurs, according to Adolph Deismann, 164 times in the New Testament. It's the phrase the Holy Spirit uses to open up to you truths about—

How as a believer you face your problems,
How you relate to God,
How He relates to you,
How you relate to others,
Where you are and where you're going . . .

This phrase encompasses the dynamics of your whole life.

The phrase "in Christ" is a succinct definition of the Christian life. When you get a clear picture of *where you are*—in Christ—you see how to live, and you get comfort and strength to do it.

Our family used to go to Cape Cod every summer. Many times when the tide was low we looked eyeball to eyeball at some little sea creature in his shell. He wasn't a bit afraid of us; *we* were the ones who were afraid! There we were with all our sixty-nine hundred square inches apiece of exposed skin—and all his possible bites and pinches. But he was safe. He knew, as long as he stayed retracted in that nice, strong shell, that we couldn't get to him.

And as far as all eternity is concerned, you're safe in Christ.

As far as all the hassles of your life are concerned, you're safe in Him.

As far as all your unknowns are concerned, you're safe.

As far as all the world, the flesh and the devil are concerned,—*you're safe.*

Lord, how wonderful my hiding place
  In Christ, in Jesus Christ!
Fortified am I from time and space,
Secretly secured by covering grace,
  In Jesus Christ.
    Kingdoms totter, powers crash and fall;
    Mortal schemers face a flaming wall!
    Alpha and Omega, Faithful, True,
    I am hidden safe, secure in You.

Those who seek will find the most, the best
  In Christ, in Jesus Christ;
Joy they'll find, and strength enough, and rest,
Peace within the midst of strain and test
  In Jesus Christ.
    Kingdoms totter, powers crash and fall;
    Mortal schemers face a flaming wall!
    Alpha and Omega, Faithful, True,
    I am hidden safe, secure in You.

All God's treasure-stores are only found
  In Christ, in Jesus Christ;
All the universe's silent sound,
Time, eternity, and truth are bound
  In Jesus Christ.
    Kingdoms totter, powers crash and fall;
    Mortal schemers face a flaming wall!
    Alpha and Omega, Faithful, True,
    I am hidden safe, secure in You.

Soon will sin's rebellions all be stilled

In Christ, in Jesus Christ;
Soon will hosts of heaven, amazed and thrilled,
See the ancient prophets' words fulfilled
In Jesus Christ!
Kingdoms totter, powers crash and fall;
Mortal schemers face a flaming wall!
Alpha and Omega, Faithful, True,
I am hidden safe, secure in You.

Now we're going to say something tough.

Picture us on that beach at Cape Cod. We're holding that little sea creature, and instead of staying safe in his shell, he's come right out and he's sunning himself on our hands, totally unconcerned. Now he's vulnerable to anything, everything.

If you refuse to learn what it means to abide in Christ; if you insist on living out there where you worry and you strive and you're insecure and even, like David, disobedient; if you deliberately choose to live as if you were not in Christ at all—you're totally vulnerable, and you're in deep trouble with yourself and with God.

He *commands* you to learn to abide in Him and stay there. He *requires* that you settle down and shelter yourself in Him and trust Him absolutely. He *insists on* your living your life *in Him*, with its resulting rest and joy. If you don't, He loves you too much to neglect you; He'll childtrain you and chastise you until you come *into Him*.

You need the "holy habit" of saying to the Father under any circumstances, "You are my hiding place"—saying it continually, and saying it in peace and stability and joy.

Let's look at some insights on being in Christ—to show you *how to live there,* and to give you comfort and strength as you do.

What a prospect! Lord help us all—as the two of us write, and as the reader reads.

Getting Into Christ

What a privilege to be "in Christ"! Being in Christ means forgiveness; it means we enjoy a place of cleansing, a place of comfort, a safe spot to which we may withdraw and regroup. We're safe "in Christ"--but how terrible the dangers outside of Him! Briefly look at what Jesus himself had to say about being "in Christ," and then at how the early church experienced it.

Read John 17:9-24

1. For whom is Jesus praying in this passage?
2. For what does he specifically ask in verse 11?
3. According to verse 12, how safe are believers in Christ? How does verse 15 add to this sense of safety?
4. Who is included in the prayer of verse 20? How does this make you feel?
5. How close to him does Jesus want his followers to be (vv. 21-24)? Do you think God honored this prayer? Why? What does this mean for you, personally?
6. What practical results does Jesus expect should come from believers being in Christ (vv. 21-23)? How does he think this should impact the world? Is this happening in your church? In your own life?

Read Acts 19:13-20

1. In verses 13-16, some men who were not "in Christ" tried to invoke Jesus' name to do a good work. What happened? Did their right motives keep them safe? How about using Christian vocabulary--did that help them? What do you think would have helped them?

2. Have you ever found yourself trying to do Christian work without depending on Christ? What happened?
3. What do you think frightened the people (v. 17)? Why? Was this fear good?
4. What resulted from this incident (vv. 18-20)? Do you think it would be easy to play religious games after this?
5. Imagine you were one of the seven sons of Sceva. After recovering from your injuries, what would you do? What would *you* do about Jesus?

If you are using this study guide in a group setting, close by spending some time in prayer, thanking the Lord for some of the benefits you enjoy in Christ.

In Christ denotes your position:
where He is, you are.
In Christ defines your privileges:
what He is, you are .
In Christ describes your possessions:
what He has, you share.
In Christ determines your practice:
what He does, you do.

2

The Essence of Christianity

The "Ray" half of us has a membership in an athletic club here in Newport Beach, our home town. It has special privileges. You can't even get into the building unless you're a member. The owner of the club is our friend John, a Christian, who says he's been greatly helped by Ray's ministry as speaker on the "Haven of Rest" radio broadcast. That's why he's been nice enough to give Ray a free membership.

But Ray's just as much a member as those who've paid the price. He walks straight through the door, and no one throws him out. He lifts weights. He runs the track. He uses the jacuzzi. He showers. He's "in."

In the eyes of that athletic club, there are those who can come in and use the facilities, and there are those who can't: the "ins" and the "outs." It's not whether the club likes some people more, or admires them more—it's simply a matter of who's a member and who isn't.

In God's eyes, as well, there are "ins" and there are "outs." It's not whether He loves some people more than others—He loves them all. But to be "in Christ" there's a cost: Christ's salvation, through His death and resurrection. By His paying the price Himself, He offers free membership to all. But some accept and some don't, so some are "in" and some are "out."

What a shame it would be if Ray never took advantage of his membership. And what an insult to John, who was kind enough to give it to him! But what a far worse loss for believers who are "in," as far as membership goes, but who never, by an act of their own will, *walk in, come in,* and enjoy all the privileges and facilities God offers to those who are in Christ!

Maybe one reason they don't is because they're untaught. They have no idea what the benefits are or how to "walk in." Strong, in his *Systematic Theology,* says that the doctrine of being in Christ is the central truth of all Christianity, and yet the most neglected.

Listen—the heart, the inner kernel, of Christianity isn't knowledge. It isn't church loyalty. It isn't ethics. *The essence of Christianity is the life lived in Christ.*

Move out beyond a mere intellectual knowledge of a historical Christ. Move even beyond accepting His payment of death on the cross for your sin, so that your name is on God's membership list.

Those two little words "in Christ" probably better define you as a Christian than any others, and no other description of you has ever had such lofty meanings or such far-reaching implications.

By an act of your will and by your daily experience, begin to live and move and have your being *in Him.* As Huegel says it, "Dispossessed of your own life, become . . . possessed of a Divine life."[1]

---

1. F. J. Huegel, *Bone of His Bone* (Grand Rapids, Mich.: Zondervan Publishing House, 1980), p. 7.

The New You

"An odd thing often happens on one of those trips into space," says the *San Diego Union* (May 19, 1973). "Several astronauts have talked about it afterward." Frank Borman said it was the "final leg in my own religious experience." Rusty Schweickart said, "I'm not the same man." James Irwin came back saying, "I want to tell people about . . . the message of Jesus Christ."

Few of us can go to the moon, but all of us need to back off, pretend we're outside of ourselves, and get eternity's view of ourselves as Christians. We need to distance ourselves from our nitty-gritty, day-by-day living and get the big picture, the scope of what it means to be in Christ.

When the apostle Paul wrote his letters, he used the phrase "in Christ" so often, you'd think early printers would have run out of "i's" and "n's". Out of his nine general letters, in six he described his readers as "in Christ." Whether they were carnal and weak like the Corinthians, or mature and strong like the Philippians—whatever their spiritual condition, Paul says that's where they were: in Christ. It doesn't have to do with how godly you are; if you're a believer, you qualify . . . you're *in Him.*

Do you know how important your position in Christ really is? Do you realize how radically new you are as a result? "If anyone is *in Christ*, he is a new creation; the old has gone, the new has come" (2 Corinthians 5:17, italics ours).

Your being placed in Him has forever changed you and has forever changed everything concerning you.

"The old has gone." Think about it. In God's eyes—and more than you have realized—the old temper you struggle with is ancient history; your old, unworthy goals are as good as gone; your old carelessness and selfishness are doomed; you are now and forever IN CHRIST.

"The new has come." Dissect that in your mind. In God's eternal record you have about you new goodness, new control, new wisdom, new compassion, new horizons of faith and becoming and accomplishing—all because you are placed IN CHRIST.

A New Perspective

Jesus Himself germinated the idea of your being in Him in John 14 and 15. Then Paul brought it to full flower and made it the color, the flavor of every part of Christian living:

You're to marry only "in the Lord."

Children are to obey their parents "in the Lord."

Joy, sorrow, triumphs and suffering are all "in the Lord."

"If there is any consolation in Christ."

"My fellow workers in Christ Jesus."

"Your labor is not in vain in the Lord."

Baptism is "in Christ Jesus."

"I am persuaded in Christ," says Paul.

Greetings "in the Lord."

"My brother in the Lord."

" . . . whom I love in the Lord."

"We have every good thing in Christ."

"Blessed are those who die in the Lord."

"Because believers are rooted in Him," says *The Daily Walk*, "built up in Him, dead with Him, risen with Him, alive with Him, hidden in Him, and complete in Him, it is utterly inconsistent for them to live a life without Him. Clothed in His love, with His peace ruling in their hearts, they are equipped to make Christ preeminent in every walk of life."[2]

Be "in Him" for your relationships. ("Lord, you have

2. *Daily Walk*, November 30, 1986 (Walk Thru the Bible Ministries, Inc., P.O. Box 80587, Atlanta, GA 30366).

put ________________________ into my life. How can I bless him/her in every contact? How can I grow and how can I help him/her grow, as we relate to each other?").

Be "in Him" for your righteousness. ("Lord, help me to accept your chastening to burn away my unpleasant characteristics and strengthen my traits and my deeds that please you.")

Be "in Him" for comfort. ("Lord, I accept grief in my life as from Your hand. But don't let me grieve as those who have no hope. Praise you that your name is Comforter!")

Be "in Him" for guidance, deliverance, healing, help. ("Lord, in this situation, in each circumstance of my life today, may my reflex action be instant prayer, instant fleeing to you.")

Abide in Him—for everything good and wonderful for you.

Be constantly affirming, "Lord, you are my hiding place."

Your Position in Christ

One of the tours to Israel the two of us have led included a time in Switzerland. Our overnight in a Swiss hotel was the high point. It was winter in the Alps, and we warmed our tummies with a wonderful supper before a roaring fire. Then to bed . . . with a leisurely breakfast the next morning before swimming in the hotel's luxurious indoor swimming pool. The water was deliciously warm. But two of the four walls were solid glass, with snow piled outside against the bottom of the frames, and a view of mountain slopes in the distance, and skiers swooping down out of the heights and passing just a few feet from our windows. We watched it all—Alps, snow, and skiers—submerged in the warm waters of the pool.

Just as it made all the difference in that Swiss hotel—in what we wore, in our behavior—whether we were "out" in the snow or "in" the pool, so being "in Christ" makes all the difference in your Christian life. All your equilibrium as a Christian, all your true understanding of relationships and destiny and functions, comes from understanding ***where you are.*** When you ***understand where you are,*** what it means to be in Christ, you'll understand how you're to be equipped and what you're to do as a result.

Paul never actually defined the term "in Christ"; we don't have to, either. He simply *used* it, over and over, until you see all its glorious ramifications. It was never a cliché, but a kind of shorthand for many facets of the Christian life.

What does being in Christ imply?

It implies incredible closeness to Him. When you're in Christ, you are a part of Him, you are connected with Him. You can't get any closer than that!

Paul knew that in a Roman prison, on a storm-beaten ship, at Caesar's judgment hall—wherever he was, all was well. Why? Because "in him we live and move and have our being" (Acts 17:28). Much later, Tennyson put it this way:

> Speak to Him, thou, for He hears,
> And spirit with Spirit can meet.
> Closer is He than breathing,
> And nearer than hands and feet.

If you're feeling at this moment that God is far away from you, we're not on the subject of "feelings." Never base what you believe on what you experience, but only on what God's Word says is true. Whether you feel it or not, Christian, *God is close to you and you are close to God*—closer than close.

If that thrills you, it's true.

If it doesn't thrill you, it's still true.

As you learn to walk by faith and not by sight, a deep sense of peace and well-being will begin to pervade your soul. You'll know, like Paul, that ***wherever you are, all is*** well—because you are close, close to Him. You are IN HIM.

Being "in Christ" implies the meeting of all your life-needs. "My God will supply all your needs," says Philippians 4:19, " . . . in Christ Jesus." So no more discarding situations when they don't "meet your needs". You come to live at ease with imperfections because, behind the scenes, your deepest needs are being totally met—in Christ. You may change jobs or cities—but not because of unmet needs. Even a Colosseum with lions becomes possible—because *you know where you are,* and you are drawing deeply from your Source.

"In Christ" implies protection. We know a mother and her two daughters who are allergic to so many substances in this world that for a long time they had to live in a special house in the woods, built and furnished just for them.

We've read about children born without immune systems who've lived in plastic bubbles to keep germ-free.

Being in Christ, in the spiritual realm, is the protection you need against everything evil and harmful in this world.

"What?" you're saying. "Will I never have a car accident? Will I never lose a loved one? Will I never hear any bad news?"

Living in Christ begins "between the ears". It involves living from the inside out. It starts with attitudes. It has to do not so much with your circumstances, but with *how you react to* your circumstances. That's the arena for real living.

The psalmist said:

> "[The man who walks in God] will never be shaken . . .
> He will have no fear of bad news;
> his heart is steadfast, trusting in the Lord.
> His heart is secure; he will have no fear" (Psalm 112:6-8).

God puts a hedge about the righteous person—as He did Job (Job 1:10). That hedge is *being in Christ.* There, he knows that nothing can touch him that a perfect and loving Father hasn't planned for his highest good. God says to him, "Have I not commanded you? Be strong and courageous. Do not be terrified; do not be discouraged, for the LORD your God will be with you wherever you go" (Joshua 1:9). When you come to understand the invisible shield continually around you when you're abiding in Christ, it will make a tremendous difference in your life.

We have friends, a Christian bookstore owner and his wife, who have had a disastrous year. Behind their backs, an inept buyer put them $100,000 in debt. At a bookseller's convention the wife had a serious fall. She's had many months of bronchitis and now she has a bad case of shingles. She writes to us, "Other than all this, life looks pretty good!"

In all the years we've known them, these two have exhibited a serenity from abiding in Christ. They don't run from their troubles, they face them with faith.

The Bible says to expect troubles: "Don't be surprised," says Peter. "Consider it pure joy," says James. And over and over it says, "Fear not, fear not, fear not." "Wait on the Lord." "Trust in the Lord."

When you come to understand the invisible shield continually around you, you'll abide in Christ with joy and rest in your heart.

Your Life in Christ

What will your life look like if you abide in Christ?

When bad circumstances threaten, you won't get the jitters—you'll pray,

> "Keep me safe, O God,
> for in you I take refuge" (Psalm 16:1).

When you're plagued with guilty feelings, you'll go back to His promises: "No one will be condemned who takes refuge in him" (Psalm 34:22). "Therefore, there is now no condemnation for those who are in Christ Jesus" (Romans 8:1).

This was true for our friend Mark, who wrestles with a thousand insecurities. He was raised in an orphanage, has no knowledge of where he came from or who, humanly speaking, he is. Even in the orphanage he was despised and finally he ran away. Nameless, penniless, colorless, Mark has become renowned, rich, colorful.

Inside, his human tendency is to degrade himself, to worry and wonder and push too hard and think it's never enough. Without Christ Mark could have become suicidal. But he continually gives his inner terrors to Jesus; to pray with Mark is a tremendous experience. His position "in Christ" has flung up a taut, straining, but joyous sail and given him full-speed-ahead power.

In times of trouble you'll relax in Him:

> "The LORD is a refuge for the oppressed,
> a stronghold in times of trouble" (Psalm 9:9).

We acted emotionally a while back. Without taking time for prayer, we cosigned for a friend's loan, which Proverbs says never to do. Then the friend went bankrupt, and the lending institution cleaned out our life savings.

For several years we thought we'd lose even our home. We had to admit, "Lord, we sinned. We asked for it; we deserve to lose it." But it was wonderful what a refuge He was! We nestled in His arms. (Probably it helped that ministry kept us too busy to think much about it.)

When someone's maliciously going after you, you'll burrow deeper into Christ:

O LORD my God, I take refuge in you;
save and deliver me from all who pursue me
(Psalm 7:1).

In the third of our twenty years pastoring Lake Avenue Congregational Church, three women decided we were pro-Communist. They wrote letters to all three thousand members—including all the missionaries who hadn't been home yet and who worried over their new "liberal" pastor. They delivered to the door of every member a petition to have us removed; they brought us before the governing board.

Through that difficult year we never defended ourselves (1 Peter 2:21-23; Isaiah 53:7). Now looking back, we see how God not only delivered us, but how He used that time to bind pastor and people together.

Yes, when your reputation is wrongly threatened, your defense will be in Christ:

Guard my life and rescue me;
let me not be put to shame,
for I take refuge in you (Psalm 25:20).

In times of danger you can be absolutely lighthearted:

But I will sing of your strength,
in the morning I will sing of your love;
for you are my fortress,
my refuge in times of trouble (Psalm 59:16).

In short, *in Christ you can be unflappable*:

He alone is my rock and my salvation;
he is my fortress, I will never be shaken.
My salvation and my honor depend on God
(Psalm 62:6, 7).

There in Christ, at last, you see where your joy is to come from:

Let all who take refuge in you be glad;
let them ever sing for joy (Psalm 5:11).

The Old Testament calls Him a refuge, a fortress, a stronghold; the psalms are full of this thought. We count sixty-one times there that those words describe Him—in addition to other psalms that say, "The Lord's unfailing love surrounds the man who trusts in him" (Psalm 32:10), "In the shelter of your presence will you hide them" (Psalm31:20); "You have been our dwelling place" (Psalm 90:1); "He who dwells in the shelter of . . . will rest in the shadow of . . ." (Psalm 91:1), "I hide myself in you" (Psalm 143:9).

The New Testament spells out the specific name of this mighty refuge—it's Jesus! Halleluia! Even more specifically, it's Christ, His name of resurrection and power.

In the glorious terms of the New Testament gospel, you and I are *in Christ Jesus.*

You're in Him the way a baby's in the womb—but better.

You're in Him the way a future butterfly's in a cocoon—but better.

You're in Him the way a deep-sea diver's in his diving suit—but better.

You're in Him the way a bird's in the air or a fish is in the water—but better.

Being in Christ means you've been placed by God in a new environment—as James Stewart says, "transplanted into a new soil and a new climate—and both soil and climate are Christ."[3]

Or we could say that being in Christ means your life and His glorious life are now totally meshed. "You are in me,

3. James Stewart, *A Man in Christ*, (New York: Harper and Row), p. 157.

and I am in you" (John 14:20). You and He are "in" each other—fused, inseparable, identified by God as one.

If the study of being in Christ is new to you, the knowledge of it will expand your mind to grasp more of "so great a salvation," and the practice of it will begin to color all your living. This truth is essential, foundational. You build your life on it.

As you study you'll understand more of the magnificent scope of Christ Himself. Whoever heard of being "in Abraham Lincoln" or "in Shakespeare"? When you come to see that you're "in Christ," you see Him far above the most towering persons of history.

When Martin Luther wrote about being "in Christ" he said, "We feel like children learning to speak. We can only speak in half-words and quarter-words when we talk about it."

God takes a poor sinner and, by His lavish grace, saves him and places him in Christ. It will take all eternity to find out totally what that means. But, we know it means that you can truly say, *"O Lord! You are my hiding place."*

Getting Into Christ

The two little words "in Christ" probably better define you as a Christian than any others. Your being placed in Him has changed you forever--you are now inseparably close to Him, divinely protected by Him, and eternally alive through Him. Consider again some of your new rights and privileges in Christ, and what they mean for you today.

Read 1 Peter 1:3-9

1. Although Peter doesn't use the term "in Christ," he does explain how we gain that standing in verse 3. How does he describe it?

2. What benefit comes with being a Christian, according to verse 4? In what four ways is it described?
3. Who is shielded by God's power (v. 5)? How?
4. Look at verses 6-7. How can believers be both "safe" and liable to hardship? What is the purpose of trials?
5. The benefits mentioned in verses 3-7 relate primarily to the future. What benefits are there for those in Christ right now (vv. 8-9)? Are you experiencing these? Why or why not?

Read Ephesians 2:11-22

1. According to verse 12, what five things are true of those outside of Christ? Which of these things most troubled you before you became a Christian?
2. What practical benefits came to the Ephesians because of their new standing in Christ? Which are true of you?
3. Why do you think Paul reminded the Ephesians of their life without God? Would your own life of faith be helped by remembering your own pre-Christian past? How?
4. If you had to pick out of this passage the one privilege of being in Christ that most encourages you, what would it be? Why?
5. Pretend for a moment that you are a hymn writer. Spend a few moments to write a single stanza thanking God for the privileges He gives us in Christ as described in this passage.

If you are using this study guide in a group setting, close by having at least some members read the stanzas they have written.

God is love:
when you're in Christ
you walk in love
(Ephesians 5:1).

God is light:
when you're in Christ
you walk in light
(Ephesians 5:8).

God is wisdom:
when you're in Christ
you walk in wisdom
(Ephesians 5:15).

~ 3 ~

One with Christ

The two of us were in Brazil on one recent Good Friday, and we went to the central plaza of the great city of São Paulo. We were among some thirty thousand people who watched a pageant of the events of that first Good Friday: the arrest, trial, and crucifixion of Jesus. The young fellow who played the part of Jesus was beaten and humiliated and actually tied to a huge cross; his body sagged in obvious pain. We were shocked when, as he hung there for most of an hour, vendors came through the crowd loudly hawking candy and ice cream. We thought, *How realistic!* and we remembered Lamentations 1:12, "Is it nothing to you, all you who pass by?"

But that man was only role-playing. Had he died in the process, he couldn't have saved himself or anyone else.

God does not see the Christian life as role-playing. His Word says that the believer's life is not an imitation of Christ; it's an actual participation in what He has done, is doing, and will do.

Take this in, absorb it, live by it: You participate in His life, and He participates in yours. Your life as a Christian is one with Christ's life. In God's eyes you are totally merged with, identified with, Christ.

Your Oneness: a Fact

Your life is not a life distinct from Christ's life. Of course this is mysterious—so don't wait until you understand it to believe that it's true. "Seeing is believing" doesn't apply to Christianity. Just the opposite: "Believing is seeing."

Your life really is not separate from the life of Christ. When He saved you, He didn't reach down from heaven and touch you with a magic wand while remaining remote and aloof.

He didn't model righteousness for you, so you could try to imitate Him and "do what Jesus would do" while He stayed in front of you, just out of reach.

He didn't save you so He could be merely some kind of Chairman of the Board of your life, or Copilot, or Skipper of your Ship, or even your Best Friend. If He had, you could indeed pray, "Lord, be with us."

He is with you, always, forever.

He is over you, caring.

He is under you, strengthening.

He is behind you, protecting.

He is in front of you, guiding.

He is within you, living His life; and you are within Him, living your life. In saving you He used an approach none of us could ever have thought up: He became one with you, inseparable from you, fusing His life with yours and yours with His, He in you and you in Him.

Says Stuart Briscoe,

> In Christ God and man are united, not as a river

> is united with the sea, losing its personality; but as a child is united with the father, or a wife with the husband, whose personality and individuality are strengthened and increased by the union.[1]

You are always you—and yet you're simultaneously in Christ. Christ is always Christ—and yet He's simultaneously in you.

Christ insists on this kind of love with you, this kind of breathtaking closeness.

Let's look at seven "togethers" in the Scriptures that show our amazing identification with Christ.

1. We were crucified together, Romans 6:6.
2. We died together, Romans 6:5.
3. We were buried together, Romans 6:4.
4. We were resurrected together, Romans 6:5.
5. We ascended together, Ephesians 2:6.
6. We are seated together in heavenly realms, Ephesians 2:6.
7. We will be glorified together, Romans 8:17.

How Are We One?

God has invented the most incredible word to explain the oneness you have with Christ. He uses it in 1 Corinthians 12:13 when He says that all believers have been ***baptized*** by one Spirit into Christ.

Not all believers have been baptized with water (the thief on the cross, to start with, and many more since then), so since this verse says "all," it must be referring to more than water baptism.

The Greek word is *baptizo,* and principally it means "to immerse" or "to envelop." The noun form means "an

1. Stuart Briscoe, *The Fullness of Christ* (Grand Rapids, Mich.: Zondervan Publishing House, 1965), pp. 51, 52.

element which has power to influence or change that which it envelops.[2]

Or it refers to one thing being brought under the transforming power or influence of another.

One Greek-English lexicon says *to baptize* means "to immerse, to plunge, to drench, to overwhelm."[3]

When you've said about a person overwhelmed by a problem, "Well, he's getting his baptism," you're agreeing that he's totally occupied with the problem and deeply affected by it.

Jesus used the word to refer to His death: "I have a baptism to undergo [and He would be totally affected by that baptism of death, becoming sin for us], and how distressed I am until it is completed!" (Luke 12:50).

Using the word positively, the Holy Spirit has "overwhelmed you" with the love and grace of Christ. He has enveloped you in Christ for the purpose of your complete, eternal transformation; He has overpowered you, He has *baptized* you into Christ.

According to the deepest meaning of the word *baptizo,* you aren't momentarily dipped into Christ, to go in and out of Him. You're truly immersed, submerged in Him, never to be taken out again. Water baptism is a precious, God-given sacrament. But if water baptism were the ultimate picture of the meaning of the word *baptizo,* every Christian would drown.

What is your true identification, you who read this? Is it that you're a woman, a black, a banker, a bricklayer, or the spouse of someone famous? Is it that you have a rare

2. This, plus more on this subject, can be found in *Intersections: Crossroads in the Gospel of Luke* (Waco, Tex.: Word Books, 1979, 1988) pp. 46, 47.

3. Arndt and Gingrich, ed., *Greek-English Lexicon of the New Testament,* (Chicago: University of Chicago Press, 1957), p. 131.

disease? Is it that you once won a great athletic championship or played in Carnegie Hall? Is it that you're in line to be an astronaut or a U.S. president, or that you're soon going into a convalescent home?

No, your identification isn't what you used to be or what you hope to be or even what you now are "in the flesh." Those things mean little, for good or bad, compared with your eternal, incomparable stature and importance and value being in Christ.

How Does Our Oneness Affect Us?

The two of us fell in love on our very first date, a moonlight horseback ride one August evening. We were both students at the University of Redlands in California. We went home that very night and wrote our parents that we'd found our marriage partners—even though we didn't tell each other.

On December 9 we sealed our desire to marry with Psalm 34:3 (KJV)—"O magnify the Lord with me, and let us exalt his name together"—and became officially engaged with a ring on Christmas morning. We dated every chance we got. We were truly, truly in love.

A year and a half later we married. Our hearts and lives began to lock together in lifelong identification. We shared one name. We became one flesh. We lived at the same address. We shared the same income, the same budget, the same bank account, the same relatives and friends. We began to share the same experiences.

Soon we shared the products of our very own love: Sherry, Margie, Ray, Jr., and Nels—and we shared the tasks of rearing them, financing them, and guiding them to their separate points of adult independence. Together we prayed, we cried, we laughed, we forbade, we commanded—and we suffered the push-pull of opposite opinions on how to do it all.

Throughout these married years we shared the adventures of new life-experiments, the exhilaration of achievements and the humiliation of defeats.

Today our identification is still certainly official, but after all these years it's much more than that. We are completely under each other's influence and power. We are truly subject to each other. We are deeply changed by one another. We are totally identified in each other's character and work. We know intimately each other's bodies, and much of each other's souls. We wouldn't dream of deliberately defying the other's wishes or of hiding major secrets. The implications of our oneness have become too many to count. We are bonded.

But *baptizo* means far more. This Greek term exposes depths of identification that married partners have never thought of. In infinitely more profound ways, *baptizo* describes how the Spirit brings you under the power and character and influence of Christ, not just for a lifetime but for eternity. As believers we are mysteriously bonded to Him, enveloped in Him, "baptized" into His life and work until we're changed totally, unalterably, and forever.

In this mysterious, glorious way you're made eternally one with Christ. Paraphrasing the way Martin Luther said it,

> All that Christ has now becomes your property; all that you have becomes His property. Christ possesses every blessing and eternal salvation; they are henceforth your property. You possess every vice and sin; they become henceforth the property of Christ.[4]

An embryo shares the body and life and nourishment of its mother. A branch shares everything in common with the

---

4. Author's paraphrase of Martin Luther as quoted by A. J. Gordon, *In Christ* (Chicago: Moody Press, 1872), p. 16.

vine. No illustration ever says it all, but you now share everything with Jesus Christ. Your life mingles with His life, and you are given fullness in Him (Colossians 2:10)—the same fullness that He shares with the Father (Colossians 1:19). You are powerfully, totally baptized into Christ.

Our friend Phyllis worked for many years as a missionary in the jungles of Mexico among Indians with almost a stone-age culture. She had no electricity, no running water, no transportation.

One furlough Phyllis helped care for a woman dying of cancer. The woman finally died, after which her widower John fell in love with Phyllis. Eventually the two of them were married.

Phyllis is no longer a missionary in the jungles. John was a globally famous surgeon, and Phyllis now shares everything John is and has. She shares his home, his connections, his wealth, his fame. Now he's retired and she shares his new lifestyle, his travels, his leisure, his interests, and his friends. She bears John's name, and her life mingles with his life. Her identity is his identity.

But Phyllis's new life is not nearly as radical a promotion as yours in Christ.

How Great Is Our Oneness?

Your life in Christ lifts you into a place vastly larger than seen at first glance.

You see, it didn't just begin when you were born again. You were chosen in Him, says Ephesians 1:4, before the creation of the world. You may well ask, "How could I be in Christ—how could God choose me and love me—before He ever made me?"

God isn't caught in time, as we are. He is over all, outside of time, seeing the end from the beginning. So He can pronounce in Revelation 13:8 that Christ is "the Lamb that was slain from the creation of the world." Events are events—and God doesn't think "when" and ask "which came first," the way we do. To Him an act is an act, and it's just as "done" before it appears on the time-line of history as afterward.

So if you're a believer, to God you've always been in Christ. Don't amplify this with human logic; you could go into heresy. Just receive it simply as truth, believe it like a little child, and rejoice in awe and wonder that it's true.

Seeing your position in Christ, you'll begin to understand how deep, how thorough, how far-reaching and how important your salvation is to God and to you. This was no willy-nilly decision you made one day, and God, seeing you turn to Him, decided on the spot to forgive your sins and accept you into His family. This was no spur-of-the-moment experience (though it may have seemed so to you) that made God look down and decide to give you one more chance.

It's true that the event of your conversion really did have to happen. One day you repented of your sins and took Christ to be your Savior.

There is a gate called Salvation, open to everyone who, of his own free will, decides to walk through it. Over the top of the gate is written in big letters, "Whoever will may come." So your Christian life had a definite beginning time, whether you remember it or not.

When you voluntarily walk through that gate and turn around and look back, on the top of the inside of the gate are written these words: "Chosen in Him." It's one of God's unexplainables, which someday we'll understand.

But meanwhile, believe that it's true. When the Holy Spirit baptizes you into perfect oneness with Christ, that's an eternal act.

Your baptism into Christ lifts you, with Him, into God's eternal scheme of all things.

> So near, so very near to God,
> Nearer I could not be,

For in the Person of His Son
  I am as near as He.
So dear, so very dear to God,
  Dearer I could not be;
The love wherewith He loves His Son
  Is the love He has for me.

"In Christ" is not a slogan to catch your attention. It's not on the level of "Things go better with Coke." It's not an additive to make your Christian life a little better, like putting extra vitamins in your milk.

"In Christ" is the very shape of Christianity's scheme of things.

It's the truth you celebrate.

It's the ground you stand on.

It's the heritage you claim.

You can't rephrase it; you can only live it and enjoy it.

It's the reason you thrill at the thought, *"O Christ, You are my hiding place!"*

Getting Into Christ

The believer's life is not an imitation of Christ's, but an actual participation in what He has done, is doing, and will do. Christ is within you, living His life; and you are within Him, living your life. He is one with you, inseparable from you, fusing His life with yours. Take one last look at how this is possible and how it changes everything.

Read Romans 6:3-13

1. You might say this is a "dead" passage. The idea of death appears at least sixteen times in these eleven verses. What things are said to have died? Would the effect be the same if

Paul had said these things were "unconscious" instead of "dead"? Why? What is so important about being "dead"?

2. Why does Paul state that Christians *are* "dead" in verse 8 and then encourage them to *consider themselves* "dead" in verse 11? You don't have to encourage corpses to act like they're dead; they can't do anything else. So why this command for Christians?
3. What advantages does Paul think dying brings (vv. 6-7, 10-13)?
4. Imagine that you had to teach the principles of this passage to someone who had no concept of death. How else could you express the ideas it presents?

Read Acts 5:12-42

1. What similarities do you note here between the actions of the apostles and the actions of Jesus as reported in the Gospels? List them.
2. What similarities do you note here between the way people treated the apostles and the way they treated Jesus? List these.
3. What do you think of the advice Gamaliel gave in verses 35-39? Is it valid? What implications would this have for those who are in Christ?
4. Gamaliel was the tutor of the apostle Paul (Acts 22:3), but perhaps the great apostle was asleep during some of his lessons. Compare Gamaliel's words in 5:39 with those of Jesus in Acts 9:4-5. What impact do you think these Damascus road words had on Paul regarding what it means to be "in Christ"?

If you are using this study guide in a group setting, you may want to divide into two groups, each studying one of these two passages. End by summarizing to the other group what each discussed.

It is one of the great principles of Christianity [says Pascal], that everything which happened to Jesus Christ should come to pass in the soul and in the body of each Christian.

A. J. Gordon,
In Christ

4

In Christ Crucified

We had a bunch of letters to mail the other day, and Ray put them into his Bible so he wouldn't forget to mail them. But his Bible went from his hand into his briefcase, and his briefcase went with him aboard a plane to Fresno, California, where he was to speak. When he got to his hotel and opened his Bible, out fell those letters. They were *in* his Bible—so everything that happened to his Bible happened to them.

In the same way, Christian, you are *in* Christ Jesus, and everything that has happened to Him has happened to you.

This makes you more involved in the cross of Christ than you may have first realized. Many Christians' only comprehension of His crucifixion is that the penalty for their sins was death (Genesis 2:17; Romans 5:12), and that God gave His only Son Jesus to pay that penalty for them (John 3:16).

So far they're right and those truths are wonderful. But then do we just walk away scot-free, brushing off our hands? Do we just say, "Thanks a lot, Lord"—and that's the end of it?

Those two little words *in Christ* open the door to much more than that. When Christ died, you and I died. Whatever happened to Him is counted as happening to us.

> Don't you know that all of us who were baptized into Christ Jesus were baptized into his death? (Romans 6:3).

Remember that God's ways are outside of and above the events of history and time. He doesn't look at the crucifixion as an event that's far away because it happened long ago—and neither must we. Morally and spiritually the cross is equally close to everybody, an ever-present reality.

What does the cross mean to you today?

It's true that Christ died that you might live, but it's also true that He died that you might *die*. This isn't something you *try* to do; your baptism into Him is so complete that when He died, you died.

After Romans 6:3 makes this bold pronouncement that all who were baptized into Christ were baptized into His death, the next verse goes on to make it clear that you went with Him right into the tomb: "We were therefore buried with him" (verse 4). Remember, Jesus didn't just swoon or faint. He actually became dead and was put into a grave. His death was a true death.

Since all that has happened to Him has happened to you, in a very real sense God, the divine Coroner, pronounces you legally dead. That's the absolute, clear-cut end of you—for a new beginning in Christ.

You're dead to two things: to sin and to the law. Let's examine these two, from Romans chapters 6 and 7.

You Are Dead to Sin

This is what Romans 6 says:

> What shall we say, then? Shall we go on sinning so that grace may increase? By no means! We

> died to sin; how can we live in it any longer? (verses 1, 2).

A look at an alcoholic helps explain this. Every time he passes a certain bar he stops in and drinks until he's out cold. How is he going to be helped over this? What can ever break his habit?

There's one sure cure: death. When he dies, he'll never drink again. You could run a bottle right under his nose and he wouldn't respond. You could wheel his coffin right by the door of the bar, his friends could all be calling to him—and he'd never move. Alcoholism can follow him only as far as death; then he's free.

When Christ died, you died. Those things that once had a grip on your life have no further right to you. Sin may call you, try to cling to you, but you need no longer be distracted.

"Well," you're saying, "maybe I don't need to be distracted by sin, but I *am*!" What we're going to say next is crucial to your faith-life (and is very little followed today).

Don't shape your Christianity from your human observations, experiences, feelings; shape it from God's Word.

God says you are dead to sin (Romans 6:1-8). And then, knowing we'll question that, He commands us to consider it true: "In the same way, count yourselves dead to sin but alive to God" (verse 11).

Only when you accept what He says will His truth begin to change your life. Then, at last, sin will no longer have the upper hand over you (verse 12), to distract and tempt and hassle you.

The point is to *believe God* when He says you're dead to all that, and you're free.

Before his conversion Augustine, who became one of the great Christians of the early church, had been quite a rounder. One day he went back to his old neighborhood and one of his former girlfriends saw him and cried, "Augustine! I haven't seen you for so long!"

Augustine began to run from her. The girl called, "Augustine! Don't you remember me? It's I!"

"Yes," Augustine called back, "but I am not I!"

Augustine had died to that old life, and it had no more claim on him. This is exactly what Romans 6 says:

> For we know that our old self was crucified with him so that the body of sin might be rendered powerless, that we should no longer be slaves to sin—because anyone who has died has been freed from sin (verses 6, 7).

You have a clean break with the past. You're truly emancipated from your old slavery to self. God has made this act so radical, He describes it as death for you. The pre-Christian part of your life is crucified; it's finished; you're dead to sin.

Tell yourself that there is an impassable gulf—a gulf as wide and deep as death—between you and what you once were. "*Reckon* yourselves to be dead unto sin."[1]

You Are Dead to the Law

That is, you're dead to all the Old Testament system of requirements which nobody ever had the power to keep.

Romans 7:1-6 pictures the power of the law. Let's illustrate it with a woman in a bad marriage. She's a slow person—easy-going, well-meaning, but sloppy. But her husband, the law, is neat, meticulous, and demanding. And the problem is, he's always right!

He comes home and says, "Dear, the dishes are unwashed, the bed's unmade, and dinner's not ready. What do you have to say?"

1. James S. Stewart, *A Man in Christ* (New York and London: Harper and Brothers), p. 188.

Well, she'd meant well, but she just couldn't seem to get it all together. She cries, and she says, "I wish I could do better."

"All right," he says, "we're going to solve this. I'll make you a schedule:

8:00-8:15, make beds;
8:16-8:46, do the dishes;
8:47-9:06, pick up around the house . . . "

And so on. He schedules her whole day, and the schedule is a productive, good one. He's right in all that he asks, and she wants to do it.

The next day she starts in, but by 10:00 she realizes she's hopelessly behind again. She sat too long over her coffee, and she can't find the list he made; and somebody called her on the phone, and she's frustrated for the rest of the day.

And he comes home.

"Did you do this?"

"No."

"Did you do this?"

"No."

Day after day they try the schedule, and day after day she miserably fails. Pretty soon she's singing that old song,

"Why don't we get along?
Everything I do is wrong;
Tell me, what's the reason
I'm not pleasin'
You?"

Now, Romans 7:2 says, "By law a married woman is bound to her husband as long as he is alive, but if her husband dies, she is released from the law of marriage."

And when this poor woman dreams of getting out of her bad marriage, a thought comes to her . . . but, oh, no, she mustn't think that . . . and she feels guiltier than ever.

And you say to yourself, "I'm always feeling guilty! I see what I'm supposed to do, but I just don't always do it. And I know the things I shouldn't do, but I catch myself doing a lot of them! There's no hope for me."

You're like this woman married to the law. But the law isn't going to die; God gave it to us, and it abides forever, and it's good. Then are you stuck? How can your impossible marriage to the law be dissolved?

Well, *you* could die. Oh, but that would ruin everything, wouldn't it? No, that's exactly the answer. God says that as a believer you're married to the law, but the truth is, you're a terrible wife. You can't measure up. You don't have the power.

So God pronounces you dead to that husband—dead to the law. "Now, by dying to what once bound us, we have been released from the law so that we serve in the new way of the Spirit, and not in the old way of the written code" (Romans 7:6).

That's the miracle of your salvation. Christ's death on the cross is also accounted as your death. And when you're dead, you're released from the law's demands. Halleluia!

Do you begin to see what good news, what a comfort, death can be?

And what is spelled out here in Romans is a theme that echoes again and again throughout the Epistles: "You died, and your life is now hidden with Christ in God" (Colossians 3:3). "Since you died with Christ to the basic principles of this world, why, as though you still belonged to it, do you submit to its rules?" (Colossians 2:20). "One died for all, and therefore all died" (2 Corinthians 5:14). Paul is bold, defiant, and jubilant about it.

You Are Crucified with Christ

Well, so far your death sounds pretty good.

God pronounces you dead to sin. Hey, you can handle that!

And God pronounces you dead to the law. What a tremendous relief! What a weight off your back!

Don't be afraid, then, to go into the deeper implications of what it means to be dead as Christ was dead. *God is good; He is kind.* Believe that, trust Him, and let's press on.

You share His death, says Romans 6:5, because you've been united with Him. It uses a Greek word for *united* that isn't used any place else in the New Testament. It literally means "grown together."

We used to live in a home in California with a famous back yard. There a former occupant had experimented with crossing blackberries and raspberries until he came up with a new breed: the California boysenberry. Two berries had been "grown together" until they became one.

The King James Version translates Romans 6:5 saying we've been "planted together in the likeness of his death."

"Grown together," "planted together"—this picture of our being united with Christ in His death makes you think of John 15, where we're called a branch and Christ the vine, or Romans 11:17, where we're called a branch that's been grafted. When you picture your being grafted into Christ, you see a deeper dimension to your identification with Him in death.

When a branch is grafted onto a stock on which it's going to grow, both must be cut. There's no grafting without wounding.

The tree must be cut. The inner life of the tree must be opened up and laid bare if it's to receive and take to itself that foreign branch. The branch must be cut, too—cut to fit the cut in the tree, so that the two wounds can be put together with the closest possible fit, and then bound and held there until they receive each other and become one.

The Lord Jesus was wounded and opens Himself up to us fully, saying, "Abide in Me. Stay close, so you can receive my life and my nourishment and all my blessings, and so that the two of us may be perfectly joined."

We can't dictate how it's to happen. We can't say, "I'll come—but I'm the executive type, O Christ. I'll take your blessings, but let me keep my 'self' intact."

No, we must "share in the fellowship of his sufferings, *being made conformable to his death*" (Philippians 3:10, italics ours). We must be cut, too—and cut to fit.

You see, that foreign branch didn't just materialize out of thin air; it grew first on another tree. It had to be cut from its original stock before it could begin to abide in the new place.

Paul wrote how the Thessalonians turned "from idols to serve the living and true God" (1 Thessalonians 1:9). They cut themselves away from one in order to be grafted into the other. It was an event; it was also a process.

You can be sure there was some pain involved.

"You've done *what*? You've decided to go to synagogue where that crazy Paul is preaching? You'll split up our family! You'll ruin our Sabbaths!"

"You did *what*? You burned that precious idol that's been handed down in our family for three generations? What will Aunt Demetria say?"

The cutting—"from idols, to God"—involved suffering. Don't think that His is the only sacrifice. "The sufferings of Christ flow over into our lives" (2 Corinthians 1:5).

The early apostles were often thrown into prison for preaching Christ—and they would leave "rejoicing because they had been counted worthy of suffering disgrace for the Name" (Acts 5:41).

Stephen was martyred by stoning. James was put to death with the sword. Paul was stoned and left for dead, and thereafter went in and out of trials and imprisonments until the end.

And he wrote to the Philippians, "It has been granted to you on behalf of Christ not only to believe on him, but also to suffer for him" (1:29).

James, half-brother of Jesus, wrote, "Consider it pure joy, my brothers, whenever you face trials of many kinds" (James 1:2). Peter said, "Do not be surprised at the painful trial you are suffering, . . . but rejoice that you participate in the sufferings of Christ" (1 Peter 4:12, 13).

> "They climbed the steep ascent to heav'n
> Through peril, toil, and pain:
> O God, to us may grace to giv'n
> To follow in their train!"

You may not suffer physically, or you may. There have been more martyrs so far in the twentieth century than in the first. The point is, we shouldn't expect that the servant will be greater than his lord.

Recently a Wycliffe translator finished sixteen years of work translating the New Testament into the language of a Himalayan tribe in a distant Buddhist country. Eleven copies of the work were brought quietly across the border, and at a cottage dedication the translator and a few tribespeople gathered. The translator recounted something of the cost involved: For each one of the thousand pages of that New Testament he had spent six days in studying, writing, and struggling with the language; and for each page he had traveled 125 miles by plane, seven miles in a small aircraft and three miles on foot. The tribesman who helped him had traveled many more miles on foot and spent many more nights in the open than he had.

And the translator reminded the people that for each page of that precious New Testament, they themselves had spent six and a half days in prison.

At the ceremony the first copy of the Testament was given to the helper, and the translator read what he had written in it:

> This book I give to you, my dearly beloved friend, from the depths of my heart. From the day we first met, you and I have traveled together sharing sorrows and joys. In all those years I have not found another like you, my friend, full of faithfulness and unflinching in difficulty. Sometimes we traveled long, long roads with loads on our backs in the scorching sun; sometimes we bivouacked deep in the snow, stiff from the cold. Never did I hear you complain. You and your friends suffered far more than we as a family ever did. You were subjected to ridicule and beatings. For the Lord's sake you were despised and bound with chains in the darkness. But in all that, because you could see the footprints of our Saviour, you broke out into songs of joy, and you even prayed for those who persecuted you. . . .
>
> You who were the last have become the first. Though men of this world count you as nothing, you count as the greatest in the kingdom of God. So then it is to you, the bravest of the brave, the most faithful of the faithful, and more honorable than the high-born, that I and my family give this Book from the depths of our hearts.

The translating helper stood to receive his treasure and clasped it to his chest. Then, weeping, he responded, "As Simeon of old waited for the Saviour in the temple and then was ready to die, so I, too, have waited long for the completion of this book, and today it is fulfilled. I hold in my hands the salvation of God for our people. Whether I die or live makes no difference now. My hopes are fulfilled, my heart is satisfied. Today, God has come not as a Jew, but as a K . . . tribesman."[2]

Never forget that the center point of all Christianity is the cross. And it's not a cross for one lone Martyr only, while all the benefactors of His sacrifice brush off their hands, say "Thanks a lot, Lord," and demand "the good life." How ugly! How vulgar! There is an identification with Him which, if we miss, we miss it all.

"We preach Christ crucified" (1 Corinthians 1:23).

We "have been crucified with Christ" (Galatians 2:20). "Those who belong to Christ Jesus have crucified the sinful nature with its passions and desires" (Galatians 5:24).

"May I never boast except in the cross of our Lord Jesus Christ, through which the world has been crucified to me, and I to the world" (Galatians 6:14).

A Christian organization recently advertised in a magazine for workers with this ad: "Wanted: Lamps to burn for God. Oil provided free." That's the way it is. Live in Christ—by Christ, through Christ. It's cheap and meaningless for a Christian to live any life except the authentically Christian life.

O my Lord Jesus on the cross, You are my hiding place.

Getting Into Christ

Christ's death on the cross is accounted as your death, too. When you're dead, you're released from all the demands of the law which you could never keep. On the other hand, in another sense you're very much alive—you're grafted into Christ, sharing His life, including both the glory and the suffering. How does this touch you? Take a closer look!

2. Story passed on to us by our dear Wycliffe friend Cal Hibbard.

Read Romans 7:1-6

1. How does Paul say someone may be released from the authority of the law? Are there any exceptions?
2. What would be your condition before God if you were not dead to the law? How does Paul say you die to the law?
3. What was the purpose of dying to the law, according to verse 4?
4. What was God's purpose in having you become the property of another (v. 4)? Is this purpose being fulfilled in your life? Why or why not? How can you tell?
5. Paul distinguishes between "the new way of the Spirit" and "the old way of the written code" in verse 6. Does the way you live your life seem more in step with "the new" or "the old"? Why do you say that?

Read Acts 9:1-22

1. Why was Ananias so reluctant to welcome Paul into the church? How would you have reacted? If you had to advise Paul on the best way to gain acceptance in the church, what would you have said?
2. What did the Lord predict about Paul's future in verses 15-16? How might this prediction relate to you?
3. What specific changes took place in Paul's life from chapter 8 of Acts to chapter 9? List them. How is this an illustration of Romans 7:1-6?
4. What do you think accounted for Paul's boldness in preaching Christ (vv. 21-22)? How

could he be so unconcerned about his own life?

If you are using this study guide in a group setting, close by reading in unison Colossians 4:3-6, Paul's prayer for this very boldness in witnessing (if you have more than one translation, use the most common one). Then pray for your own boldness.

The believer's life is . . . one with the Saviour's . . . It is not a life running alongside His, and taking shape and direction from it. It is His life reenacted in His followers, the reproduction in them of those events which are immortal in energy and limitless in application.

A. J. Gordon,
In Christ

~ 5 ~

In Christ Risen

At the age of eight our son Nels was playing Little League baseball. In his division that year the winning team was the Padres (six wins and one loss). Their standing was number one; they were the champions. And Nels was *in* the Padres. He was *in* that particular team.

It didn't mean he'd lost his personal identity. He was the only one named Nels Ortlund and he had his own particular function: He played outfielder. And believe me, even though all the little guys wore blue uniforms and caps, you can be sure his parents in the bleachers could pick him out from the rest of the team!

Because Nels was *in* the Padres, he was considered a winner. Because the Padres were champions, Nels was a champion, too. "In" his third grade class or "in" Sunday school he might be something else. But "in" the Padres—no matter how poorly he might play on a given day—he was number one.

So with you, "in" Christ. You may be having a bad day, you may feel down on yourself. But you're identified with a winner—and in Christ you're a winner, too!

A Winner with Christ

We think of *with* as an external word. A physical education teacher says, "Now, do this *with me*," and teacher and student work side by side. So we're apt to pray, "Lord, be *with me*."

But it's not like that with Him. You won't understand "with Christ" until you understand "in Christ." When Romans 6:8 says you died "with Christ," it's not as if you were another thief on a separate cross who died with Him side by side. No! Because you are "in Him" you have common organic functionings. When you graft new skin onto a body, the new skin takes on the rhythms and the metabolism of the body.

This is why, *in Christ*, everything that happened to Him happened to you. You are one *with Him* because you are *in Him*. Living *in Christ* means living out the life of Christ.

God didn't leave His Son hanging on a cross—and neither does he leave you experiencing only being crucified with Him and nothing more.

> We were . . . buried with him through baptism into death in order that, just as Christ was raised from the dead through the glory of the Father, we too may live a new life. If we have been united with him . . . in his death, we will certainly also be united with him in his resurrection (Romans 6:4, 5).

Wonderful! Every day of your life you're an Easter Christian!

"Christ . . . is your life" (Colossians 3:4). Of course that means that you take Him in all the experiences of your life, and He shares them with you. But more. It also means that He takes *you* in all the experiences of *His* life, and you share them with Him.

Soar we now where Christ has led,
Following our exalted Head;
Made like Him, like Him we rise:
Ours the Cross, the grave, the skies.

"Ours . . . the skies." Read it in Ephesians 2:4-6:

> Because of his great love for us, God, who is rich in mercy, made us alive with Christ even when we were dead in transgressions—it is by grace that you have been saved. And God raised us up with Christ and seated us with him in the heavenly realms in Christ Jesus.

The two of us travel constantly, ministering together, and most of the time we fly. We enter the plane, we buckle up, and soon we're soaring thirty thousand feet high and five hundred miles per hour toward our destination. All the passengers are flying together. It's not just *our* flight, meaning the Ortlunds'; we're all in the plane, all aboard fly.

So in Christ we believers are all raised together and seated together with each other and with Him.

This is mystery; this is miracle. You are seated in heavenly realms more surely than you are now seated on a chair. Temporal things are passing away; the unseen is the true. The more you absorb and understand this mystery-miracle life God has given you, the more you'll take advantage of it and let its power and authority shape your daily living.

Risen in Christ

Think with us about your resurrection in Christ.

First let's illustrate it this way. When God created the world, He created it with history already built in. The stars, and also the light from the stars—that light that takes thousands of light years to get to earth—everything was created in one act. God created it "old."

When He created man, He created him, too, with history already built in. Adam was created a full adult; he didn't go through the process of growing up. He was made in an instant with an age factor already built in.

When you were born again, you were placed into Christ, and the history of Christ was accounted, was credited, to you. You were given the advantages of His history, so that the experiences that Christ Himself went through are now yours as well.

That's what Colossians 3 says; now live like it!

> Since, then, you have been raised with Christ, set your hearts on things above, where Christ is seated at the right hand of God. Set your minds on things above, not on earthly things (Colossians 3:1, 2).

"Set your *minds* on things above;" "set your *hearts* on things above." Bishop Lightfoot comments, "You must not only *seek* heaven, you must also *think* heaven."

Sometimes the two of us, if a problem comes along, say to each other, "Keep looking down!" It always brings a chuckle. If we were to say, "Keep looking up," we'd be indicating we're in the pits. But what we're doing is reminding each other of our exalted position in the heavenlies in Christ—and everything immediately looks better.

Strong in Christ

Resurrection life is now yours, available for every need, because you're in Christ. "If the Spirit of him who raised Jesus from the dead is living in you, he who raised Christ from the dead will also give life to your mortal bodies" (Romans 8:11).

Life is actually translated "vitality" in the Phillips paraphrase. It's not future; it's here-and-now miracle life, translatable into everyday vitality for your present mortal body. The new life which He gives you, called *zoe* in the Greek, is a new kind of life altogether. It's not earthly life intensified, it is the life of the post-resurrection Christ. It has the quality of eternity about it. You are really alive!

Karl and Luella Van Vorst were members of our church in Upper State New York. The year they were engaged, Luella got severe polio. They were married at her bedside in the hospital.

We knew them two sons and thirty years later, and for all those years they had both lived on resurrection power. Karl never complained. There was always a twinkle in his eyes. He ran a dairy farm, he dressed Luella and combed her hair, he got her in and out of cars and chairs and bed, day after day, year after year.

Luella never complained. She had a twinkle, too. And God certainly supplied resurrection life to her mortal body. There was almost no power in her arms, but Karl built her kitchen counters the height of her fingertips, and she learned to stand upright and cook. In her forties she finally also mastered writing. Through the years she taught thousands of Bible classes and with great administrative skill ran our large annual vacation Bible school.

Derek and Nancy Lewis also know that *zoe* life for their mortal bodies. Their first son Michael was born with the severest kind of cerebral palsy. Over the years they've fed him and lifted him in and out of his wheelchair and turned him over during the night. Derek and Nancy are both small, and Michael, now twenty, is bigger than they are. Still, triumphing over emotional pain and physical stress, Derek and Nancy are vivacious, as Romans 8:11 describes it. They live without complaining—in fact, with downright joy—the resurrection life which is theirs in Christ Jesus. And so does Michael, though he can't do much but smile and laugh.

Seated in Christ

"[God] raised [Christ] from the dead and seated him at his right hand in the heavenly realms," says Ephesians 1:20.

Superiors sit; inferiors stand in their presence. And Christ Jesus earned the right, by His death and resurrection, to sit in heaven. The book of Hebrews, emphasizing Jesus' superiority over priests and kings and angels, talks a lot about His being seated:

> After [Christ] had provided purification for sins, he sat down at the right hand of the Majesty in heaven (1:3).
>
> We do have such a high priest, who sat down at the right hand of the throne of the Majesty in heaven (8:1).
>
> When [Christ] had offered for all time one sacrifice for sins, he sat down at the right hand of God (10:12).
>
> [He] endured the cross, scorning its shame, and sat down at the right hand of the throne of God (12:2).

And in Christ you, too, have great authority. Seated "with him in the heavenly realms in Christ Jesus," His triumph is your triumph, and His place at the Father's right hand is your place.

Being seated with Christ means that you're in—

A place of honor. As the Son, "the radiance of God's glory," sits down at the right hand of that Heavenly Majesty (Hebrews 1:3), so you, in God's eyes, are radiant with the glory of Christ and share His prestigious seat (Ephesians 2:6).

A place of rest. As Christ, the great High Priest, has finished His work and can do no more (Hebrews 10:12, 13), so *in Him* you will never again have to work—that is, strive to be acceptable to Him. Away with anxiety that your church attendance, your giving, your serving might not be quite enough to earn God's favor! He says in Christ you can rest (Hebrews 4:3).

A place of learning. As the Son in His earthly life sat daily in the temple teaching (Matthew 26:55), so you, too, have an amazing "anointing" (1 John 2:27), the very "mind of Christ" (1 Corinthians 2:16).

Of course you need to study; of course a "know-it-all" attitude would be obnoxious. Actually, when we realize all God says He has given us in Christ, we can only be filled with worship and wonder.

A place of intercession. As the Son has the intimate ear of Almighty God (Hebrews 7:25), so you have that same place of unbelievable privilege, so that you can ask what you will and it shall be done (1 John 3:22; 5:14, 15).

A place of fellowship. As the Lord Jesus in His earthly life loved sitting and talking to Mary (Luke 10:39), so He does now with you!

> . . . and He talks with me,
> And He tells me I am His own;
> And the joy we share
> As we tarry there
> None other has ever known.

We can't understand it. We can only say with wonder and awe, "Lord, I came here in poverty; how did I get this wealth? I came here a humble person; how did I get exalted? I was in the dust, on an ash heap; how did I get seated with princes?" (1 Samuel 2:7, 8).

And the Lord Christ will answer,

> To him who overcomes, I will give the right to sit with me on my throne, just as I overcame and sat down with my Father on his throne. He who has an ear, let him hear what the Spirit says to the churches (Revelation 3:21, 22).

Lord, what an awesome mystery! As you are seated in the heavenlies, you are my hiding place.

Getting Into Christ

Resurrection life is yours, available for every need, because you're in Christ. It's not earthly life intensified, it's the life of the post-resurrection Christ. It has the quality of eternity about it. In Christ you have a place of honor, a place of rest, a place of learning, a place of intercession, a place of fellowship. Now, live like it!

Read Ephesians 2:4-7

1. Why did God make us "alive with Christ" (v. 4)? What difference does this make?
2. How did God make us "alive with Christ" (v. 5)? What difference does this make?
3. In what sense are believers "seated . . . with Christ" in the heavenly realms? How can you make this truth come alive in your experience? Give three examples that "flesh out" your answer.
4. According to verse 7, why are believers seated with Christ in the heavenly realms? Why do you think this is important to God? How is this knowledge to transform us even now?

Read Revelation 4:1-11

1. In your own words, describe the person pictured in verses 2-3, 5, 9. What images come to mind?
2. Some redeemed saints sit on thrones around this person (v. 4). They are obviously people of great standing; yet, note their response to the central figure of the passage (vv. 9-11). What implications does this have for those of us who cannot see this magnificent scene?

3. Imagine yourself as one of these twenty-four elders. What must be going through your mind as you witness the events this passage describes? Now connect these thoughts to Ephesians 2:4-7. How does this scene from Revelation enlarge your understanding of what Paul was driving at in Ephesians?
4. In what circumstances in your own life would it help to remind yourself to "keep looking down"?

If you are using this study guide in a group setting, sha with each other your answers to the final question. Close praying for each other.

To be 'in Christ'
is to be . . . at the depths of life,
'supernaturalized'!

Adolph Deismann

6

How Do People Get Into Christ?

This is a very important chapter, and whoever you are, you need it. You need it if you're still on the outside looking in, but you also need it if you're a long-time Christian in order to witness and pray effectively. There are perilous misconceptions these days, spread by well-meaning but faulty preaching and witnessing.

Gospel means "good news," and the essence of what people need to be received into Christ is *facts*. They need to hear the truth.

On that Day of Pentecost when the Holy Spirit came, three thousand people became Christians because they "accepted [Peter's] *message*" (Acts 2:41). Philip witnessed to the Ethiopian eunuch by first asking, "*Do you understand* what you are reading?" (Acts 8:30). *It's dangerous to ask people to experience becoming a Christian before they clearly understand the gospel.*

When Paul reminded the Corinthians "of the gospel I preached to you, which you received and on which you have taken your stand," he said, "By this gospel you are saved"—and then he defined that gospel by listing certain facts: "That Christ died for our sins according to the Scriptures, that he was buried, that he was raised on the third day," and so on. This is the message to which we must witness.

Four Common Errors

First, we're not primarily to be witnesses to all the benefits of the Christian lifestyle. Peter's and John's preaching to the crowds in Acts 3:19 was not, "Come join us in the exciting new movement that's sweeping the city. Our fellowship is where the action is. You'll love the preaching and teaching! And we eat together and have neat times." No, it was the message of Jesus' death and resurrection, and then they said, "Repent, and turn to God, so that your sins may be wiped out." Ouch!

Sins burden people in the twentieth century as severely as they did in the first, and that message was just as bold and awkward and cutting-edge-dangerous and embarrassing to the first-century mind as it would be today. But the message and the principles of the Word of God—not whatever is culturally "in"—provide the power tools needed in every age to do God's miracle work in God's way.

No wonder Satan caricatures the rare Christian willing to urge unbelievers to repent as a demented old codger on the sidewalk with a sandwich-board sign. He fears the power of this message when it's taken seriously.

Second, we're not to be witnesses primarily to the possibility of people's having some exciting spiritual experience. Christians can too hastily, with minimum input of the doctrinal facts, ask someone to "accept Jesus into his heart" and immediately expect him to feel something great. If he doesn't, he's exhorted to "take it by faith" that he's been born again—when in fact maybe he wasn't given enough of that powerful gospel for the new birth to have happened.

And when he falls away he'll be bitterly disillusioned.

Who is this Jesus you want them to invite into their hearts? Why do they need Him? Do they believe He is truly the Son of God, the One who died to redeem them from their sins? Do they believe He truly rose again and lives eternally? Are you showing them from His Word (Hebrews 4:12)?

Third, we're not to be witnesses primarily to our own personal lives—so that maybe even without any words on our part, people will admire us so much they'll ask, "What's special about you? I want what you have." Again, Satan gets us to caricature verbal witnessing by getting us to call it "cramming the gospel down their throats," to make sure we won't do it, so much does he fear its power.

(Dr. John Huffman tells of a businessman who tried this approach—letting his life do the witnessing—with a friend in his office. Finally after many months the fellow said, "Sam, there's something different and special about you. Are you a vegetarian?")

No life is good enough to represent Jesus Christ, and no life has the ability—without words—to get across the gospel, which *in itself* is "the power of God for the salvation of everyone who believes" it (Romans 1:16).

The gospel facts themselves are the power, and we must not demand that any other power accompany the simple, clear presentation of the gospel itself. It is enough.

How does a person come into Christ? "Faith comes by hearing the message," says Romans 10:17, "and the message is heard through the word of Christ"—that is, the Bible.

Fourth, we're not to witness primarily to God's filling of personal needs. The genuine gospel is Christ-centered, God-centered. It isn't centered on the needs of those who need Him. If they indeed receive Him, they must adjust their entire lives to Christ from then on, on His terms.

Notice the witnessing you see in the book of Acts. Peter used his sermon in Acts 2 to show that Jesus had risen from the dead, and his punch line was, "Be assured of this: God has made this Jesus, whom you crucified, both Lord and Christ."

Philip "preached the good news of the kingdom of God and the name of Jesus Christ" (Acts 8:12), and told the Ethiopian eunuch "the good news about Jesus" (Acts 8:35). Saul (Paul) grew powerful "proving that Jesus is the Christ" (Acts 9:22).

Too often people are urged to invite Him into their self-centered little castle to do things for them. A nominal, almost unknown Savior is expected to have some kind of power, like a genie in a bottle, to make them happy and fulfill all their dreams. A self-centered conversion experience will make a self-centered Christian. From this point on they'll spend their lives seeking counsel and input for the satisfaction of their egos. They'll expect those around them to "meet their needs." They'll be critical of their pastor or church if they feel they're not being "fed," and all their expectations will be as self-centered as their initial experience.

Truth Is God-Centered

There are deep, high implications to the story of John 3:16 that "God so loved the world that he gave his one and only Son, that whoever believes in him shall not perish but have eternal life."

God is saying, "I am a high and holy God, offended by your sin. That's why I decreed that if you insist on remaining in it, you must perish.

"But I love you with a responsible love: I love you too much to let you easily go! I'm committed to go to the end of my love to get you cleansed and back into my fellowship, joyfully restored to me for eternal life.

"That's why I've given for you my most cherished possession, my Son whom I love, with whom I am well pleased, with the only stipulation that you *believe the truth* about Him.

"I've done all I will do. The next move is yours. Will you believe?"

The facts of John 3:16 drive straight to a person's greatest need: not to be fulfilled and feel better—but to find mercy and riddance of his guilt, with its resulting prospect of death and hell. He's not just wounded and wanting love; he's most of all a sinner and lost. How can he get right with God? How can he prepare to meet Him? That's his most basic insecurity and anguish.

The cry deepest in his soul isn't to have God adjust to him; instinctively he knows he must adjust to God. And if he wins when he's presented with these tough truths to wrestle, he will become a tough, clear-eyed disciple.

Here's the rub in presenting the authentic gospel: In a blame-shifting society, it demands admitting responsibility. "*I'm* a sinner. *I* have offended God. *I* must accept His salvation, on His terms, offered at the great cost of the death and resurrection of His Son, if I'm to be acceptable to Him."

This intellectual and emotional conviction can come only from the Spirit of God Himself. Said Jesus about the Spirit, "When he comes, he will convict the world of guilt in regard to sin and righteousness and judgment" (John 16:8). This is why, on the front line of battle, it takes the courageous use of the spiritual weapons of prayer and the Word to see souls wrested from the Enemy and brought into Christ.

But how wonderful it is for people who've been running to doctors and pills and experiences and therapists—anything to rid themselves of the damning torture of guilt—for these poor souls to face the reality and cause of the guilt itself, and then be led to the only One whose death and resurrection can effect their perfect forgiveness and healing! Oh, the release, the joy that comes!

Our job, fellow Christian, isn't to make the gospel easy, but to make it clear.

The Power of the Truth

Paul sums up how the Ephesian believers got "into Christ" by three steps: they *heard*, they *believed*, and they were *marked* permanently in Christ with the seal of the Holy Spirit:

> And you also were included in Christ when you *heard* the word of truth, the gospel of your salvation. Having *believed*, you were *marked* in him with a seal, the promised Holy Spirit, who is a deposit guaranteeing our inheritance until the redemption of those who are God's possession—to the praise of his glory (Ephesians 1:13, 14).

When you *hear* the gospel and *believe* it, then the Holy Spirit comes into your life to be the proof that you're now one of His. His indwelling presence says to the hostile evil forces around you, "This one belongs to me. Hands off. No trespassing here. I myself am the sign: THIS IS PRIVATE PROPERTY—*my* property." You've seen horses or cattle or sheep branded with a mark of ownership. So God marks you as "in Christ," paid for by His blood.

Paul also says it another way, that God's Spirit in you is the deposit, the down payment, guaranteeing all the rest that is to follow at your ultimate, completed salvation when you go to meet Christ.

When a person makes an offer on a large purchase, such as real estate, he is sometimes asked for earnest money. He knows he'll forfeit that if he doesn't complete the agreed sale. So the Holy Spirit placed within you is God's earnest money, His down payment, His guarantee to go all the way through the deal of your salvation. This strong activity on

His part shows how much He loves you and how totally committed He is to you in Christ.

It's all "to the praise of his glory!" It's most of all for Him. Ephesians 1:13, 14 is called one great doxology, one magnificent sentence of praise. Paul gets so excited here about the truths he's giving that he says it with a majestic contempt for grammar. This highly educated scholar, this great man of letters, stumbles all over himself trying to express the unutterable heights and depths of the gospel of our God.

This is the gospel that places people in Christ.

It's not first an advertisement of Christian benefits.

It's not primarily a promised wonderful experience.

It's not first a display of our own Christian life as "Exhibit A."

It's not first a prescription for healing the sinner's ills.

It is "the word of truth," from the pages of Scripture: the simple, powerful story of the substitutionary death and resurrection of God's Son to redeem us.

> And you also were included in Christ when you *heard the word of truth,* the gospel of your salvation (Ephesians 1:13).
>
> From the beginning God chose you to be saved through the sanctifying work of the Spirit and through *belief in the truth* (2 Thessalonians 2:13).

This is the truth that comforts millions of souls, as they cry, *"Lord, I am truly in Christ! In all the storms of this world, you are my hiding place."*

Getting Into Christ

Those in Christ are not called primarily to proclaim all the benefits of the Christian lifestyle, or to the possibility of exciting spiritual experience, or to their own personal lives, or to God's filling of personal needs. Their primary duty is to proclaim the simple, powerful story of the substitutionary death and resurrection of God's Son to redeem humankind from sin.

Read John 3:16-18

1. Why did God send His Son into the world (vv. 16-17)? With whom does the impetus for evangelism start? How does it start?
2. Why does the world need to be "saved" (v. 17)? What are the consequences of not being saved (v. 18)?
3. How does one avoid being condemned? What is the present-day status of those who do not believe in Christ?
4. What does John mean when he calls Jesus God's "one and only" (or "begotten") Son (vv. 16, 18)? What is so unique about Him? Why is this important in evangelism?
5. Why do you think John 3:16 is so well-known, even outside of Christian circles? What accounts for its power?

Read Acts 16:22-34

1. Why do you think Paul and the other prisoners stayed in their cells when the earthquake could have freed them? What does this imply about our own priorities?
2. What caused the jailer to ask his question in verse 30? And why do you think he asked Paul

and Silas, and not one of the other prisoners? What clues does this passage give about the link between the gospel *message* and a godly *lifestyle*?

3. How did Paul and Silas answer the jailer's question (v. 31)?
4. From what you know of Paul's preaching as recorded in his letters, what else do you think he might have told the jailer when he "spoke the word of the Lord to him" (v. 32)? How did this message change the jailer's life (vv. 33-34)? How has it changed yours?

If you are using this study guide in a group setting, share separately how the gospel has changed you. Close by pairing up or clustering in threes; pray for each other to have a clear witness for Christ.

When we are united to Christ, the whole of His past life is made available to us, not simply to compensate for our past (by way of pardon) but actually to sanctify our present lives, so that our own past may not inescapably dominate our present Christian life.

We, who in the past have marred the images of God by sin, may gaze into the face of Christ and discover power and holiness there on which to draw, so that the power of our own past sin may not destroy us in the present.

Sinclair Ferguson,
Know Your Christian Life

7

A Crucial Distinction

A son is a son is a son. He can be a bad son or a good son, but he's a son. His "state" at any one moment may be rebellious or obedient, miserable or content—but his "standing" in the family is unchanged; he's a son.

Once you're truly born again into the family of God, you can't be unborn—even though you can become wayward and be a great grief to your Father.

The parable of the prodigal son in Luke 15:11-32 illustrates this. Jesus said this fellow was one of the family's sons. He was just as much a son when he was in the distant country as when he was at home. He was just as much a son after he'd spent all his inheritance as when he still had it. He was just as much a son feeding pigs as when he enjoyed his family's lifestyle. His standing was never jeopardized, even when his state was terrible!

Did the father receive him back as an outsider to be reinstated into the family? No, not by any means! He received him as his dear son seeking restoration. Long before he had reached home the father was there with love to meet him.

Still, the son had really "blown it." He had missed a whole period in his life that could have been like his older brother's, to whom the father said, "You are always with me, and everything I have is yours." The father had a feast prepared for his loved younger son—but that's not to say that son didn't live from then on with the embarrassment of those rebellious years and all the money wasted, and the regret of having caused his father so much grief.

In your standing before God, because of His powerful salvation, you are pure, perfect, without blemish in His sight. But if you choose to rebel you can accumulate a lot of scars. This explains why God's Word is so full of warnings and guidance toward "the good life."

Your Standing in Christ

Let's look at three negatives which help explain your perfect standing in Christ.

First, your standing in Christ is not progressive.

Let's take a six-year-old child who trusts in Jesus. His understanding of the faith will grow, of course; but that child is no less "accepted in the Beloved" than Christians who've walked with the Lord sixty years. You're accepted by the virtue of Christ, not because of your longevity.

Or take an adult who's known the Lord for only a month. He's no less a Christian than an old timer. His sins are just as forgiven; his destination is just as sure.

Ephesians 1:5 says that every Christian is adopted into full sonship. Two meanings for "adoption" are possible: One is the way we understand it today; the other was a Roman custom similar to being "Bar Mitzvahed." Up to a certain age the child was considered a minor member of the family—loved and cared for, but without much status or responsibility. He was trained and schooled and disciplined and held under until the day of his adoption, the day when the father decided he was mature enough to be considered an adult son (see Galatians 4:1, 2). At this point, with great celebration, he was "adopted"; he became a full heir to all the father's holdings and accepted as a man in the family.

How different from that when you came into Christ! At the moment you were born into God's family you were adopted without any probationary period at all! Immediately He gave you the full privileges of adult sonship. Amazing!

That is why we say your standing is not a condition into which you progress; it's a position in which you're placed. It can't be improved on.

Second, your standing in Christ is not a sensation or an experience.

It's not anything you feel. God *declares* you His child. He *declares* that you're in Him. He makes an eternal decree that when you believe in Christ you are placed in Him.

In a home Bible study a while back we'd been reading John 1:12:

> Yet to all who received him, to those who believed in his name, he gave the right to become children of God.

We said, "Now, how many of you would like to share with us when you received Him? Maybe it's been just recently." One of the men spoke of the time he received Christ.

There was a long silence, and finally one of the men said, "Well, I haven't gotten there yet, but I'm working at it. I guess I just haven't been hit with that bolt of lightening."

Some of us began to say, "But you don't have to wait for any experience!" We told him that coming into a right standing with God doesn't happen that way; it's simply assenting to the facts about Christ and submitting to Him in all the implications of those facts.

That evening our friend quit waiting for the "big bolt" and believed in God's Son, and at that instant, God placed him into Christ.

Numbers of people are waiting for some kind of tingle in their spines before they're saved. God is not in the entertainment business! He's interested in people's salvation.

Third, your standing in Christ is not a reward to be earned.

You may be a good son or daughter or a bad son or daughter. Your position as God's child isn't conditioned on your behavior. It's dependent on Christ, as you believe that He did everything necessary to save you and you put your trust in Him.

There are four things that would have to happen for you to lose your standing in Christ once you are placed there by the Father.

Someone would have to snatch you out of His hand. But Jesus gives a picture in John 10 that indicates you're tenderly enclosed in the hands of both the Father and the Son: I give them [says Jesus] eternal life, and they shall never perish; no one can snatch them out of my hand. My Father, who has given them to me, is greater than all; no one can snatch them out of my Father's hand (John 10:28, 29).

On earth, very few things seem safe. That came clear to us not too long ago when we were in Rome. There, just innocently strolling down a busy street, Anne lifted her purse strap from around her body to reach inside for a tissue. In an instant two fellows roared by on a motorbike. One steered close to her and the other grabbed for the purse. In seconds they were out of sight. The purse was gone forever.

In this life, purses can be snatched. But can anyone snatch you out of the Eternal Grip of Almighty God? Impossible!

Someone would have to break the seal of God's ownership of your life. Ephesians 1:13 gives a succession of steps in the act of your salvation:

a. You heard the word of truth;
b. You believed;
c. You were included in Christ;
d. You were marked in Him with a seal, the promised Holy Spirit.

For you to lose your standing in Christ, someone would have to break the hold of the Holy Spirit, a seal stronger than any seal on earth.

Break the seal of that all-powerful Spirit of God? Impossible!

O love that will not let me go,
I rest my weary soul on Thee.*

Someone would have to separate you from the love of Christ. When Paul in Romans 8 asks, "Who shall separate us from the love of Christ?" he answers,

> I am convinced that neither death nor life, neither angels nor demons, neither the present nor the future, nor any powers, neither height nor depth, nor anything else in all creation, will be able to separate us from the love of God that is in Christ Jesus our Lord (Romans 8:38, 39).

Separate you from His love? Impossible!

Someone would have to get up to heaven and erase your name from the Lamb's Book of life. Philippians 4:3 defines Christians as those "whose names are in the book of life." And says our almighty Savior Jesus Christ in Revelation 3:5,

* If your Christian tradition teaches other than this on the security of the believer, let's not part company and break fellowship. We realize there are problem passages in Scripture and that we don't have all the answers. Let's stay together through these studies, and we'll both come out stronger.

"I will never blot out his name from the book of life."

Erase your name from His book? Impossible!

Your State in the World

It's one thing to be a saint; that's your standing. It's another thing to be saintly; that's your state. God's part of the deal is perfect, but our part isn't.

Colossians 3:1-5 spells out the difference:

> Since, then, you have been raised with Christ [That's your standing],
>
> Set your hearts on things above [Make your present state consistent with such a standing].
>
> Set your minds on things above, not on earthly things. [Discipline your state to be worthy of your standing].

Here's your standing:

> For you died, and your life is now hidden with Christ in God. When Christ, who is your life, appears, then you also will appear with him in glory.

So let your state be this:

> Put to death, therefore, whatever belongs to your earthly nature: sexual immorality, impurity, lust, evil desires and greed, which is idolatry.

Who wouldn't want to, when God gives us such a standing? How embarrassing to us, how disappointing to Him, to live as if we were still in our old life, when we realize the way He chooses to see us!

Much of the New Testament will sound like gobbledygook to you ("you died," "put to death, therefore") unless you see the difference between your state and your standing.

Recently the New York City Police Department investigated a tragic death. Sprawled in a filthy back alley lay an old bag lady who had finally lost her battle with life. For years she'd kept her body going by stealing the leftovers off plates in restaurants—but the more efficient the restaurants became, the more those food scraps were denied her. At last her frail, dirty shell gave up.

Then the newspapers revealed the news: Investigations showed she'd had many bank accounts, each holding hundreds of thousands of dollars! This old woman's *standing* was with the wealthy of the city, but her miserable *state* was that of a pauper.

Christian, do you ever live spiritually as if you were poor? Do you get discouraged, do you worry, as if you had no resources—when God has given you everything in Christ? The world is full of spiritual "bag ladies" whose states are tragically inconsistent with their standings.

Oh, that you would take comfort in Hebrews 10:14: By one sacrifice [Christ] has made perfect forever those who are being made holy.

There! Do you see it? You're already perfect: That's your standing. You're being made holy: That's your state. Both are true.

Hold up your head, Christian, take a deep breath and let God encourage you!

> Being confident of this, that he who began a good work in you will carry it on to completion until the day of Christ Jesus (Philippians 1:6).

Lord, until the Day—You are my hiding place.

Getting Into Christ

Your standing in Christ is not progressive; it's not a sensation or experience; it's not a reward to be earned. Your

standing as a son or daughter of God is forever secure, purchased for you by the precious blood of Christ. Your state is something else; it changes with your willingness to obey. It's our job to daily rely on God's power so that our state matches our standing.

Read Colossians 3:1-10

1. Divide a clean sheet of paper into two columns. On one side write the heading, "Standing"; on the other, write "State." Now go through verses 1-5 and identify which of Paul's statements relate to the Christian's "standing" and which to his "state," and list them in the appropriate column.
2. You've probably heard the phrase, "Pie in the sky in the great By and By." Is that what Paul advocates in verses 2-4? Why or why not?
3. Look carefully at verses 5, 8-9. Do any of the things named there still cause you trouble? If so, which ones? What are you doing about them?
4. What is the capstone reason Paul gives in verses 9-10 for putting aside old sins? What phrase here indicates that improvements in our state are *progressive* (v. 10)?

Read Revelation 2:18-26

1. What is the standing before God of these people of Thyatira (v. 19)?
2. What is the state of a few of these same people (vv. 20-21)?
3. What is the Lord's response to continued, willful sin in this church (vv. 22-23)?

4. What is the Lord's challenge to this church (vv. 24-25)?
5. What is Lord's promised reward for those who strive to make their state match their standing (v. 26)?

If you are using this study guide in a group setting, close by singing the first verse of a favorite hymn or song which expresses a desire to improve our state—perhaps "Fill My Cup, Lord"; "Make Me a Blessing"; or "Teach Me Your Way."

Christ Enclosed

Enclosed in Christ!
Within, above, around me,
And underneath
The everlasting arms:
Encirclement complete;
I'm satisfied, and sing.
Nothing alarms.
Enclosed in Christ!
He ever is between me
And my weakness,
My anxiousness, and loss.
And then again
I have no care, no discontent,
Nor failure,
Not even lacks;
They're all nailed to His cross.
Enclosed in Christ!
His joy, despite conditions,
Is always mine,
His victory is sure.
In Him we live, and move,
And have our being.
His power is boundless,
And will e'er endure.

Mrs. F. McQuat, "Mother Mac,"
a shut-in member of one of our churches

~ 8 ~

The Hottest Commodity This Side of the Trinity

Recently we saw a foreign family huddled on the sidewalk at the Orange County airport—obviously new refugees from somewhere in Southeast Asia. They looked so frightened and confused! Around them were a few sacks of possessions, and they seemed very much alone.

Soon all of us were relieved to spy a couple who were apparently this family's sponsors. An interpreter was along, explanations were made, and soon they all went off together. What a wonderful thing to think that here was another needy family in the world who was being tenderly received into a new country, to be given a place to stay, provision for its needs, and a fresh start in life! We commented to each other that it would take months, perhaps years, for that family to discover all the great advantages that were suddenly theirs as new residents of America.

Did you know that from the moment you believed in God's "Good News," you were transported from the kingdom of darkness to the kingdom of light? God placed you into Christ and it will take eternity for you to understand all the advantages of your new position in Him.

From the first three chapters of Ephesians alone, you see these advantages. In Christ you're:

1. Blessed with every spiritual blessing (1:3);
2. Chosen before the creation of the world (1:4);
3. Loved (1:4);
4. Predestined (1:5, 11);
5. Adopted (1:5);
6. Accepted (1:6);
7. Redeemed (1:7);
8. Forgiven (1:7);
9. Lavishly given God's grace (1:7, 8; 2:7);
10. Shown the mystery of His will (1:9, 10);
11. Given a guaranteed inheritance (1:11, 14);
12. Made "for the praise of His glory" (1:12);
13. Secured by the Holy Spirit (1:13);
14. Called to a glorious hope (1:18);
15. Made a recipient of God's power (1:19);
16. Made alive together with Christ (2:5);
17. Raised up with Christ at His ascension (2:6);
18. Seated with Him in the heavenly realms (2:6);
19. Created as God's masterful workmanship, for the purpose of good works (2:10);
20. Brought near to God (2:13);
21. Brought into a relationship of peace between Israel and the Gentiles (2:14);
22. United into one body of Christ (2:15, 16; 3:6); made a fellow citizen with God's people (2:19) and a member of His household (2:19);
23. Created for the Spirit's habitation (2:21, 22);
24. Made a partaker of God's promise (3:6);
25. Given the revelation of His mysteries

(3:8-11); and
26. Given bold and confident access to God (3:12).

Do you really comprehend all these riches of yours? Of course not. It's like gazing at the crown jewels in London's Tower; you really can't grasp all that you're seeing.

All these advantages of yours are just from Ephesians' first three chapters alone. Other New Testament references proclaim that in Christ you're:

27. No longer condemned (Romans 8:1);
28. Made a child of God (John 1:12; 1 John 3:1, 2);
29. Foreknown (Romans 8:29);
30. Called (Romans 8:30);
31. Justified (Romans 3:24; 5:1; 8:30);
32. Glorified (Romans 8:30);
33. Sanctified (1 Corinthians 1:30);
34. Made a recipient of eternal life (Romans 6:23);
35. Made a new creation (2 Corinthians 5:17);
36. Reconciled to God (2 Corinthians 5:19);
37. Made righteous (2 Corinthians 5:21);
38. Made a citizen of heaven (Philippians 3:20);
39. Made complete (Colossians 2:10):
40. Made perfect (Hebrews 10:14); and
41. Made God's own possession (1 Peter 2:9).

And there are others! One of our good friends, preaching one time on the blessings we have in Christ, exploded, "We're the hottest commodity this side of the Trinity!"

Years ago we attended a Bible conference outside Philadelphia where Dr. Donald Grey Barnhouse was to preach. Just before his message a girl sang a beautiful solo, which ended with these words:

I am satisfied with Jesus. . . .
But the question comes to me

As I think of Calvary:
Is my Master satisfied with me?

And Dr. Barnhouse came to the pulpit and shouted, "YES, HE IS! You are *in* the Lord Jesus Christ, and God is utterly and eternally satisfied with you!"

Let's narrow our Bible study to the book of Colossians. For years Christians have found delight and strength from this book. Why? What is it God says here that causes such a response?

Among other things, He lists some of the wonderful advantages that are forever yours because you are in Christ Jesus.

Advantage One: You Are His Personal Miracle

The apostle Paul begins his letter to the Colossians—and to you—with such tender and exciting words! He says,

> To the holy and faithful brothers in Christ at Colosse: Grace and peace to you from God our Father (Colossians 1:2).

"What?" you say. "I'm neither holy nor faithful. I fight bad thoughts, I sense a lot of ego in me, I lose my temper, I'm weak, I want my own way."

Remember the difference between your standing and your state! God sees not your state but your perfect standing in Christ—and you *are* "holy and faithful."

But there's more; let's dig deeper. Even looking at your present state, which seems to you so shaky and inconsistent, God says you are very special. Like a good parent who mercifully reads into his child the best, and who affirms his child ahead of time to gently nudge him to *become all he needs to become*, so God says to you, "My dear child, you are Mine, and you are already special. I have chosen you out of the world to be separate, different, set apart to become like Me. My love and my promises right now rest upon you.

Don't argue with Me. Don't fight what I'm saying. I consider you holy and faithful."

If that's truly how God sees you, then you stand taller, don't you, and you *want to become* holy and faithful in order to measure up to His generous assessment.

"Grace and peace," write Paul to the Colossians. It was his hug on paper—but more. In the warmth of his "hello" was theological truth: grace—that they were in God's grace, in the divine favor that saves undeserving sinners; and that, as a result, peace—between God and them was a cessation of hostilities—peace was declared. That's a miracle!

All the tender assurances that Paul gave the Colossians are yours as well. Like them, you came to Christ with your dark past, your great needs, your fears and insecurities and bad habits and failures. God didn't say, "Who needs you?" No, He greets you with a warm hello and every assurance of all the new advantages you have because He's placed you in Christ.

He's clothed you with Him (Isaiah 61:10).

He's housed you in Him (Psalm 18:2).

That's a miracle only God could perform!

Advantage Two: Transferred From One Kingdom To Another

> For he has rescued us from the dominion of darkness and brought us into the kingdom of the Son he loves (Colossians 1:13).

"Rescued . . . brought." "From . . . into." What a gigantic transfer!

We had a letter today from Tahlib, a handsome young Indian friend. Tahlib has been rescued from hell and brought into heaven.

Several years ago when we were holding meetings in South India, we ate breakfast together one morning in our hotel. In came this dark-looking young man and sat right down at our table, the way the "public" has felt free to do in the Middle East since Bible times (Luke 7:36-38). Our first impression was how truly dark he was. It was more than his dark skin and black hair; it was the dark expression on his face. Indeed, he had the look of one held captive by true darkness.

In his broken English he told us, "I have no peace. Lucifer tell me do suicide."

For most of an hour we talked. The son of a local doctor, Tahlib was a university student hooked on drugs and desperately unhappy. We talked about God's good news, and that day the Lord Jesus Christ transferred him from the dominion of darkness to His own kingdom.

When we saw him the next day, Tahlib broke into a radiant smile and began to repeat to us the song we'd taught the people: "In my life, Lord, be glorified!"

Ever since, Tahlib has written us faithfully and sent us presents. Over the years we've seen the confusion melt away and the stability grow. His questions have changed from "How long do I struggle?" to "Which baptism is right?" to "As a member of the Sanhedrin, was Paul married or not?" He studies his Bible vigorously. He's asking God about full-time ministry.

Today's letter includes another picture: Tahlib sitting at his desk. He's grown a beard. His teenage thinness is gone, and he looks established, happy, mature. The kingdom of light is a delightful place to settle into, and Tahlib is there!

At one time, you and I, like Tahlib, were captured by darkness.

> Long my imprisoned spirit lay,
> Fast bound in sin and nature's night. . . .

Darkness in the Scriptures has to do with Satan's spheres of ignorance, laziness, selfishness, carelessness toward the law, lust in thought or deed, coarseness, crudeness—the "low road" of living which ends in death and hell.

But—

> Thine eye diffused a quick'ning ray,
> I woke, the dungeon flamed with light;
> My chains fell off; my heart was free;
> I rose, went forth, and followed Thee.

The Greek word for *brought* in Colossians 1:13 was used in Paul's world for transferring from one country to another. *The Expositor's Bible Commentary* says it might be rendered "re-established"—like the Southeast Asian family.

And so with you, when you trusted Christ.

The other day we heard on the radio of a person who escaped mainland China by swimming toward Hong Kong. On the way a shark struck and wounded him. Someone in a helicopter saw him and came to rescue him. But as the helicopter rose up from the water a fog came in, the pilot got confused, and by mistake he landed back on mainland China!

When your Father rescues you from the domain of darkness, you'll never find yourself back there again. What He promises, He delivers. He safely transports you into the kingdom of the Savior.

Once in the early years of corneal transplants, a cornea was donated by a criminal on his way to the gas chamber. That cornea was carefully taken and transplanted into the eye of a law-abiding citizen.

Something very like that happened when God found you and you willingly said, "Lord, I believe." He took you out of that old Adam, as it were, and placed you into the body of Christ. And now you're in Him, seeing eternity and God and righteousness and sin from the viewpoint of the eternal Son of God. You're still you, but you've been gloriously transplanted into Christ.

Advantage Three: You Are Held by Him

> All things were created by him and for him. He is

> before all things, and in him all things hold together (Colossians 1:16, 17).

Never think of Jesus Christ as merely a man who "walked the dusty roads of Galilee." Friend, He *made* the dusty roads of Galilee!

He is also the Cosmic Glue. Science is mystified over why our whirling atoms don't simply disintegrate, causing all the material universe to break up in one giant conflagration.

The Lord Jesus Christ is the reason. He "holds all things together"; Hebrews 1:3 says He "[sustains] all things by his powerful word."

But more. You yourself, believer, are particularly held by Him. Your body, soul, and spirit are held, truly held. Do you know how "held" you are?

"I am always with you," prays the psalmist; "*you hold me*" (Psalm 73:23).

A thousand years later Christ nods, "Yes, I hold in My very hand *all* My children, and—

> No one can snatch them out of my hand. My Father, who has given them to me, is greater than all; no one can snatch them out of my Father's hand" (John 10:28, 29).

Christ holds you, the Father holds you. The two hands merge into one clasp, and you are utterly securc. Relax in that truth. Mentally, physically, right now rest in it. *You are held.*

"But what if I slip out of His fingers?" someone asked. And the answer came, "You *are* one of His fingers!"

Such is God's holding. Wonder of wonders, in Christ you become part of Him!

Advantage Four: You Have the Treasures of Wisdom and Knowledge

> My purpose is that [you] may be encouraged in heart and united in love, so that [you] may have

> the full riches of complete understanding, in order that [you] may know the mystery of God, namely Christ, in whom are hidden all the treasures of wisdom and knowledge (Colossians 2:2, 3).

Many a student has smiled over Psalm 119:99, "I have more insight than all my teachers," and especially hoped it was true at exam time! But actually it's a fact—if the student is a child of God and the teachers are not. Like the miracle of life stowed away within an ordinary-looking seed, "the mind of Christ" is planted within every Christian (1 Corinthians 2:16), with the potential one day soon to "know fully" (1 Corinthians 13:12).

How does it happen? Who teaches you? The Holy Spirit. John calls him the "anointing" or the "unction" God put within you:

> You really need no teaching from anyone; simply remain [or abide] in him, for his unction teaches you about everything and is true and is no lie—remain [abide] in him (1 John 2:27, Moffatt).

God places you in Christ, and God also places in Christ all the treasures of wisdom and knowledge. It seems too much to comprehend, too good to be true! But it's God's flat statement of fact.

In Paul's day pagans invented what were known as "mystery" religions. New members went through special rites of initiation and were given secrets they could never share. All this made them feel religiously superior to everyone else.

Paul snatches their very word *mystery* from Satan's use (Colossians 1:26, 27; 2:2; 4:3) and says the mystery of God in Christ is a secret open to everyone who is in Him, a secret revealed with great power and glory.

"In [Christ] are hidden *all*," says Colossians 2:3. Circle in your Bible that word *all*. There are no secrets outside of Christ; there is nothing hidden from Him, but everything is hidden in Him. And—

> It is because of him that you are in Christ Jesus, who has become for us wisdom from God—that is, our righteousness, holiness and redemption. Therefore, as it is written, "Let him who boasts boast in the Lord" (1 Corinthians 1:30, 31).

Hidden in Colossians 2:3 means to be stored away as you would your valuables, and yet be accessible for ready use. Christian, you are rich! Christ is the safety deposit box for all wisdom and knowledge . . . and you have the key!

Notice the difference between *wisdom* and *knowledge*. An engineer may be full of knowledge about his field of science; but if he doesn't have wisdom—tact and common sense in dealing with people—he'll never get to be the engineer he dreams of becoming.

A psychologist may have great knowledge of the working of the minds and emotions of people, but if he doesn't have the wisdom to handle those people, he'll never be successful.

A politician may be filled with know-how about political science, and yet not have the insights to move and lead people.

Just so may someone have great knowledge of the facts of the Bible; but only one who is hidden with Christ in God has the ability to combine that knowledge with Spirit-given wisdom. In Christ there is available not only the facts of life but the common sense to use those facts aright. All this is yours in Him.

Advantage Five: You Have a Solid Front Line of Defense

Writes Paul to the Colossian Christians,

> I . . . delight to see how orderly you are and how firm your faith in Christ is (Colossians 2:5).

These believers were very much under attack—and so are you. Like them, *in yourself* you're more vulnerable than you know; at any moment you're one short step from disaster.

But *in Christ* your line of defense is unbroken. Your faith is unshaken. In that position, your faith will never collapse; it will be orderly and disciplined.

No wonder, then, Ephesians 6:10 says, "Be strong in the Lord and in his mighty power"! As you abide there in Him, He becomes your fortress, your rock, your strong tower, your hiding place.

Advantage Six: You Have Fullness in Christ

> For in Christ all the fullness of the Deity lives in bodily form, and you have been given fullness in Christ (Colossians 2:9, 10).

Friend, you are in Christ, who is the glorious Total of God. Spiritual "poor talk" is out. "I'm not much," "I can't do that," "I don't have enough resources," "Who am I...?" are all inappropriate for a child of the King. Without Him you are nothing; but in Him you are rich, able, full, complete.

When Christ lived on earth He was the visible display of the triune God. The word *fullness* or *completeness* means that Jesus Christ was Deity running over. Colossians 1:19 says, "For God was pleased to have all his fullness dwell in him."

Who can explain God? It takes all of Jesus Christ to explain Him. There are hundreds of functions and facets and names of Jesus: the Light, the Ancient of Days, the I AM, Wonderful Counselor, the Light of Israel, the Branch, The Rock, the Lord, the chief Cornerstone, the Way, the Truth, the Life, and on and on. He is the express image of God's Person, but it takes every facet of Him to reveal fully the glories of the Godhead.

And in this way Paul says that "you [plural] are complete in him" (Colossians 2:10, NKJV). As it takes all of Christ to express God, so it takes all believers to express Christ.

This is the Christ in whom you've been placed. This is the Christ who surrounds you—above you, beneath you, around you, before you, behind you, within you. This is the Christ who is all, and in all. You are complete, "running over," in Him!

As He is now in heaven, so are you in this world. You are in His name, in His plans, in His power, in His dignity, in His authority, in His reign, in His grace. When you come to Him by faith, all this and more comes to you.

In Christ you are in that vital, dynamic, eternal environment of the power of glory. Colossians 2:7 says you are in Him as a plant is in soil—living, rooted, growing, flourishing, and drawing all from Him.

Missionary Hudson Taylor in China, after a long period of struggle in his faith, came to write this in a letter:

> The sweetest part . . . is the *rest* which full identification with Him brings. No longer is there need to be anxious about anything, for He, I know, is able to carry out His will, and His will is mine.

In Christ you have great advantages. You're God's personal miracle. You're transferred from the Kingdom of Darkness to the Kingdom of His Son. You're held secure by Him. You're given all the treasures of wisdom and knowledge. You have a solid front line of defense against the Enemy. And you're given fullness in Christ.

Maybe you're saying, "It all seems so intangible, so abstract. It just doesn't excite me."

Let us answer that with an illustration. There was a time when Ray said to Anne, "I love you. I want you to be my wife." She could have said, "But that seems so intangible—'I love you; I want you to be my wife!'" Except that she read into those words a name, a family, a house, a bank account, a friend, a social escort. It didn't seem at all intangible to her!

God says to us, "I love you, and I want to put you forever into Christ."

And you can read into that . . . everything.

> Thou, O Christ, art all I want;
> More than all in Thee I find.
>
> . . . *You are my hiding place.*

Getting Into Christ

Staggering--that's the word for our advantages in Christ. We are God's personal miracle. We've been transferred from the kingdom of darkness to the kingdom of light. We're held safe in God's almighty hands. We have available to us every treasure of wisdom and knowledge. We have an impregnable defense against all enemies. How thankful we should be for all these gifts!

Read the Ephesians "Advantage List" on pages 90-91

1. Which five of these twenty-six advantages of being in Christ mean the most to you personally? Why?
2. According to Ephesians 2:10, what responsibility do these advantages bring? How firm is God about this responsibility?

Read Acts 2:42-47

1. If you had to choose one word to characterize the life of these early Christians, what would it be? Why?

2. What advantages or benefits do you see expressed in the daily life of these believers? Do you see any similar benefits in your own Christian experience? Why or why not?
3. Which of the benefits you identified in question 2 are mentioned in the Ephesians passage just studied? How do the "doctrine" of Ephesians and the "experience" of Acts relate? How do they relate in your life?
4. In what settings did these believers live out their advantages in Christ? How is this significant?
5. How did God respond to these believers living out their faith (v. 47)? Do you think He responds that way today? Why?
6. Whenever Christmas rolls around, very often grandmas and grandpas around the world send their grandkids special presents. If you ever received such a gift, most likely your parents made you write a thank you letter. God has given all of us priceless presents of his grace. Take a few moments to write out a thank you letter to God for the gifts mentioned in this passage from Ephesians, and show it to one other person.

If you are using this study guide in a group setting, take turns sharing your thank you letter to God with others in the group. Close with a prayer of thanksgiving.

The summons of the Gospel is not that we behold what is possible for us in Christ, and reach forth to it; but rather that we behold what is accomplished for us in Christ, and appropriate it and live in it.

A. J. Gordon,
In Christ

~ 9 ~

A Crucial Choice

If a person isn't "in Christ," where is he? The Bible expresses it many ways.

He's dead in trespasses and sins (Ephesians 2:1, KJV).

He's in his sinful nature (Romans 7:25).

He's in the world (Ephesians 2:12).

He's in bondage (Ezra 9:9).

He's in Adam (1 Corinthians 15:22).

A word the Bible often uses for what he's "in"—the sum of everything that man can do by his own efforts, everything human that opposes God,—is the word *flesh.* "I know that in me (that is, in my flesh) dwelleth no good thing" (Romans 7:18 KJV).

Take off the H and spell it backward and you have *self*—and that's another way of defining *flesh.* The endless choices between the realm of God and the realm of the flesh are described from Genesis to Revelation.

"Stop trusting *in* man" (Isaiah 2:22). "He who trusts *in* himself is a fool" (Proverbs 28:26). "If . . . he trusts *in* his righteousness, . . . he will die" (Ezekiel 33:13). "Cursed is the one who trusts *in* man, who depends on flesh for his strength. . . . But blessed is the man who trusts *in* the LORD, whose confidence is in him" (Jeremiah 17:5, 7). "Whoever trusts *in* the LORD is kept safe" (Proverbs 29:25).

Every person will one day be judged on what he's "in"—in *the flesh* or in *Christ.*

Wrote Paul,

> For it is we . . . who glory *in Christ Jesus* and who put no confidence *in the flesh*—though I myself have reasons for such confidence. If anyone else thinks he has reasons to put confidence in the flesh, I have more:
>
> Circumcised on the eighth day,
> Of the people of Israel,
> Of the tribe of Benjamin,
> A Hebrew of Hebrews;
> In regard to the law, a Pharisee;
> As for zeal, persecuting the church;
> As for legalistic righteousness, faultless.
>
> But whatever was to my profit I now consider loss for the sake of Christ, . . . that I may gain Christ and be found *in Him* (Philippians 3:3-9, italics ours).

Here you see a seven-step ladder of the flesh struggling upward—a typical, rickety old ladder of human standards and human efforts. You could substitute any stepladder that climbs to blue blood ancestry or social hobnobbing or achievement, whether artistic, intellectual, or professional. It represents the best that man can do *in himself*; and his eternal choice is whether to trust *in* himself or *in* Christ.

At the end, will he discover he's in the Lord, his rock, his fortress, his refuge? Or will he discover he's in the flesh, in some sort of humanistic Tower of Babel made of his own construction?

Let's look at that very Babel Tower, and see a picture of what it's like to be "in the flesh."

"The Flesh" Goes Its Own Way

Genesis 11:1-9 tells the story of the Tower of Babel and what the energies of the flesh do. It's the story of God's second great judgment of the human race—the first being the flood, in Genesis chapters 6-9. Only Noah and his immediate family, eight members in all, survived that devastating flood.

So now it's "new beginning" time, and one family begins a second time to carry out God's original command to populate the earth (Genesis 1:28; 9:7). Genesis 10 lists the family's first descendants and their resulting people-groups. They're off to a fresh start.

Will they live for themselves—in the flesh—or will they live for God—in Him? The choice is ahead of them.

Noah's descendants soon choose to live "in the flesh." Gradually they migrate from the general area of Ararat (Genesis 8:4) to the sun belt, a plain in Shinar (Genesis 11:2)—the plain of Babylonia, situated between the Tigris and Euphrates rivers, toward what is today the Persian Gulf.

That's an area with definite potential for (materialistically speaking) "the good life." It was famous in antiquity for its extreme fertility and excellent irrigation. Archeologists suggest 4000 B.C. as the time these people actually settled here, and possibly it took another century before they'd multiplied sufficiently and developed industries and art to enable them to build a city.

Now, there is absolutely nothing wrong with the good life when it's God-given. There is everything wrong with it if it's man-acquired, by his own efforts, for his own ends, apart from God.

"The Flesh" Has Great Capabilities and Potential

At that time "the whole world had one language and a common speech" (Genesis 11:1).

This unity of speech gave the people incredible potential for accomplishment. Think of the disarray and distrust in the world ever since, simply because people misunderstand each other! Think of the cumbersomeness of doing business in the world or of trying to cooperate and unite in any way. Think of the agony of trying to spread the gospel. The two of us travel constantly in our ministry to foreign countries, and we see it. It's very hard to cross language barriers.

But the post-flood world was fresh and new, with every advantage and every potential. Said the Lord Himself, "If as one people speaking the same language they have begun to do this, then *nothing they plan to do will be impossible for them*" (verse 6, italics ours).

At that time they broke through to a new invention: They started baking their bricks (verse 3), which gave the bricks such rock-like strength and hardness that even today there are great remnants of ancient buildings made of these bricks. The potential of these people was enormous.

"The Flesh" Opposes God

Though they knew God's express command to multiply and to scatter over the earth (Genesis 1:28; 9:1), now the people said, "Why should we scatter? Why should we 'call on His name' as in the old days (Genesis 4:26)? Let's make our own name! Let's exalt ourselves. Let's compete with God!"

> Come, let us build ourselves a city, with a tower that reaches to the heavens, so that we may make a name for ourselves and not be scattered over the face of the whole earth (Genesis 11:4).

The flesh isn't interested in sacrifice and service. "The flesh" wants to please itself, look good, get ahead of everybody else.

"Let's get together and build a skyscraper right up to heaven." Both Babylonian and Assyrian kings are on secular record as priding themselves on the height of their temples, having tops as high as heaven. And God's own condemnation of "the king of Babylon" in Isaiah 14 includes these words:

> You said in your heart,
> "I will ascend to heaven;
> I will raise my throne
> above the stars of God;
> I will sit enthroned on the mount of assembly,
> on the utmost heights of the sacred mountain.
> I will ascend above the tops of the clouds;
> I will make myself like the Most High" (vv. 13, 14).

This is "the flesh." It's the old I-am-the-master-of-my-fate-I-am-the-captain-of-my-soul mentality. It's the spirit that wrote on the side of the Titanic, "Not even God can sink this ship!"

"The flesh," whether in old form or modern, raises itself in arrogance and boasting, without taking into consideration God, or dependence on Him, or fear of His judgment.

"The Flesh" Leads to Destruction

So in this ancient land the flesh rebelled against God, and He confused the people's tongues to diffuse their power and force them to scatter. "And they stopped building the city. That is why it was called Babel" (Genesis 11:8, 9). *Babel* sounds like the Hebrew word for "confusion," and we get from it our English word *babble*.

Babylon not only historically represents rebellion against God, but symbolically as well. At the end of time, in Revelation chapters 17 and 18, Babylon, called "the great prostitute" (17:1), symbolizes all that is "in the flesh," all that is opposed to God—rich and wicked and finally doomed by His judgment.

What a tragedy the Tower of Babel was! Those early builders wanted to be "in" their own creation with their own identity, rather than "in" the Lord and with His identity. They tried to be safe in themselves instead of safe in Him.

"The Flesh" Plagues Even Christians

The flesh is still your danger and mine. Until heaven, the "old nature" of the flesh is still inside us, and we Christians have the death-struggle described in Romans 7:14-25, the choice between living in the flesh or living in Him. We either do all we can do to preserve ourselves, exalt ourselves, coddle ourselves, strengthen ourselves, and store up for ourselves for the future, or we choose to *abide in Him,* and to lose ourselves because we trust Him totally.

The choice is self-preservation or sacrifice, being "in" self or "in" Him, survival or service.

Carnal or worldly Christians live "in the flesh." Non-Christians live "in the flesh" because it's all they have; how terrible if Christians choose to join them and also live in the flesh instead of relying on all their great resources in Christ! Then their goal is simply survival, building their Babel towers, maintaining themselves, keeping themselves intact no matter what the cost. Despite any appearance to the contrary they are basically centered on self.

Churches, denominations, any kind of Christian group may also choose to live in the flesh. They can build their own Towers of Babel, refuse to spend themselves in blessing the world. They're not giving themselves away for the sake of the lost around them, they're simply maintaining themselves and their buildings. They're keeping up their organizations. They're desperately hanging onto their doctrinal distinctives and lifestyle distinctives and old traditions. They're concentrating on *surviving*—and that's a sad thing.

The church working at survival doesn't know it's already dead. Its pastor and people are busy counting their members and fussing with their budgets and seeing if they have more baptisms than rival churches and trying to keep in the good graces of headquarters. All that is survival business. They're dead before they're dead!

Secure Ones Can Risk

But a Christian (or a church) who understands that he's truly *in Christ* knows he *does not need to survive,* that he's expendable. He knows only God's will matters—that churches or organizations or individuals can come and go as God pleases, but that he's eternally safe *in Him.*

People say, "But, after all, you've got to *live*!" No, you don't. All the most precious things of this world have been paid for by those who were willing to be expendable.

All the apostles died as martyrs, but they left to us a great legacy of truth.

John Wesley died financially poor but rich in blessing.

Borden of Yale gave away his great wealth and died while a young man, but he lives on powerfully in the history of missions.

David Livingston gave his life for Africa, but he influenced his entire world.

The Lord Jesus didn't come to earth to survive, He came to serve. He came not to save Himself, but to sacrifice Himself for others. He modeled it, and He said it:

> The man who loves his life will lose it, while the man who hates his life [that is, is deliberately

> indifferent to his own welfare if the needs of God's program require it] . . . will keep it for eternal life (John 12:25).

Survival is not his concern—*God* is his concern. And God says this is the one who actually survives.

The early descendants of Noah had to decide whether they'd build a great tower with their newly-invented bricks and so seek to preserve themselves, or whether they'd submit to God's order to scatter like seeds all over the earth and trust God to preserve them. That's our choice, even as believers: to live "in the flesh" or to abide in Him. We must decide whether we'll "do the best we can" to preserve ourselves, or whether we'll risk and spend ourselves.

We can afford to risk and be spent. We're absolutely secure in Him. Christian, you are in Christ. Abide there!

> The name of the LORD is a strong tower;
> the righteous run to it and are safe (Proverbs 18:10).

Understand that, live like it, enjoy it. Say to Him, *"Lord, You are my hiding place."*

Getting Into Christ

What is the flesh? Take off the H and spell it backwards and you have self, a pretty fair definition. Trust in the flesh, and you're headed for trouble; stay there too long, and you die. Even Christians can be troubled by the flesh. Men and women in Christ must make a continuous, conscious decision to resist the flesh and rely solely upon the power of Jesus. It's a battle!

Read Romans 7:15-25

1. Have you ever felt the way Paul describes

himself in verses 15 and 19? When was the last time you felt like that?

2. Paul almost sounds like he's ducking blame for personal sin in verses 17 and 20. Is that really what he's doing? What do you think he means?
3. In our "I'm OK, You're OK" culture, it's not often that you hear people talk about themselves as Paul does in verse 18. Why is this admission a healthy and necessary part of Christian growth?
4. Paul says in his "inner being," in his core self, the part that is really and truly Paul, he delights in God's law. Can you say the same thing? What does this mean for you?
5. What is the only way of escape from the flesh, according to Paul (vv. 24-25)? How do you take advantage of this way?

Read Acts 8:9-25

1. How would you describe Simon's spiritual condition before the coming of Philip to Samaria? What sort of man was he?
2. What soon happened to Simon, according to verse 13?
3. What do you think motivated Simon's proposition to the apostles as recorded in verses 18-19?
4. In your own words, restate Peter's reply to Simon in verses 20-23. What response did he want?
5. What does Simon's final request in verse 24 imply about his spiritual state? His standing?

If you are using this study guide in a group setting, close by pairing off and sharing with each other one weakness in the flesh; then pray for each other.

"As long as Christ remains outside of us, and we are separated from Him, all that He has suffered and done for the salvation of the human race remains useless and of no value to us."

John Calvin

10

Out of Danger and Into Christ

For the first time it began to rain. Nobody had ever seen it rain before. It rained for forty days and nights without let-up, until the rivers swelled and flooded over, the valleys filled to their brims, the people climbed and climbed and climbed. They stood on the mountains' highest peaks and the water swirled around their knees, up to their waists, up to their chests, up to their mouths. . . .

This was the situation for the whole world at the time of Genesis chapter 6. Would all creation drown? Well, God is a God of amazing grace and mercy, and He loves to rescue those in danger if their hearts will turn to Him.

Let's look at the ark of Noah and see how God prepared a refuge, a place of safety, for all those willing to believe in and take advantage of His terms of rescue. See how the ark is a picture of what it means today for you to be hidden from danger "in Christ."

Noah's Ark

God is not only a God of mercy but of justice, and you

can be sure that people outside of Him don't get away with deliberate sin forever.

When there is widespread sin, widespread judgment threatens. There have been, and will yet be, times when God's patience runs out. Although "the wages of sin is death" (Romans 6:23), God takes "no pleasure in the death of the wicked, but rather that they turn from their ways and live" (Ezekiel 33:11). So "He is patient . . . not wanting anyone to perish, but everyone to come to repentance" (2 Peter 3:9). God waits and pleads and gives new chances for repentance over and over and over. There are eight hundred such pleas in the Bible.

A good gardener, if he discovers blight killing his favorite rosebush, will cut the plant almost to the ground to save the stock and give it new hope. When our loving God saw moral corruption threatening to destroy the precious people He had created, the time came when, in love, He had to "cut them down almost to the ground":

> The LORD saw how great man's wickedness on the earth had become, and that every inclination of the thoughts of his heart was only evil all the time. The LORD was grieved that he had made man on the earth, and his heart was filled with pain. So the LORD said, "I will wipe mankind, whom I have created, from the face of the earth..." But Noah found favor in the eyes of the Lord.
>
> So God said to Noah, "I am going to put an end to all people, for the earth is filled with violence because of them. I am surely going to destroy both them and the earth. So make yourself an ark" (Genesis 6:5-8, 13, 14).

When widespread judgment threatens, God offers mercy. God saw a man! Amid all the corruption he saw a bit of healthy stock that could be salvaged to begin again His human race: "Noah was a righteous man, blameless among the people of his time, and he walked with God" (Genesis 6:9). He wasn't sinless but he was blameless; he had a heart after God.

God made an inconceivable prediction: "I am going to bring floodwaters on the earth" (6:17). Even though it had never rained, Noah simply believed that whatever God said was true. He acted on two little words: "trust and obey." Says Hebrews 11:7, "By faith Noah, when warned about things not yet seen, in holy fear built an ark to save his family. By his faith he condemned the world and became heir of the righteousness that comes by faith."

God's judgment is never too harsh. Don't ever underestimate the patience of Almighty God. It took 120 years to build that ark, a boat with the capacity of a freight train thirteen-and-a-half miles long! All the time Noah was building, he preached and pleaded with those around to repent (2 Peter 2:5 calls him a "preacher of righteousness"). First Peter 3:20 confirms this by saying that "God waited patiently in the days of Noah while the ark was being built."

It seems as if God's great heart of love delays judgment to the last possible moment. In Genesis 7:1-4 He told Noah to go into the ark because in seven more days—not immediately—the rain would begin. The people had a whole week to view in living color the protection of the ark with its inhabitants inside; it was just a matter of *believing God* when He warned of coming destruction.

As Hebrews 11:7 says, Noah's very faith, his simple reliance on the Word of God, condemned the unbelieving world of his day. Of their own free will they condemned themselves. They refused to walk through that ark's wide open door.

But God's salvation is on his terms and for a limited time only. There was only one door into that ark of safety, and through that door came fleas and elephants, ants, tigers, and people. It was available to all, though all had to come the same way.

But then the awesome moment arrived at the end of God's forbearance and patience, *He Himself shut the door* (7:16). Divine judgment then wiped out all life except that which was *in the ark,* God's merciful provision for salvation.

God's present plan of salvation will eventually terminate. Jesus taught at His first advent that a second day is coming when God's patience will run out—and it will also come with seeming suddenness:

> Just as it was in the days of Noah, so also will it be in the days of the Son of Man. People were eating, drinking, marrying and being given in marriage up to the day Noah entered the ark. Then the flood came and destroyed them all (Luke 17:26-27).

Peter wrote that this next judgment will not be by water but by fire:

> By these waters . . . the world of that time was deluged and destroyed. By the same word [of God] the present heavens and earth are reserved for fire, being kept for the day of judgment and destruction of ungodly men. . . . The heavens will disappear with a roar; the elements will be destroyed by fire, and the earth and everything in it will be laid bare" (2 Peter 3:6, 7, 10).

Concerning that awesome day, Revelation 22:10 says "the time is near." And then it follows with these sobering words, when God has again "shut the door" and it's too late for anyone else to repent:

> Let him who does wrong continue to do wrong; let him who is vile continue to be vile; let him who does right continue to do right; and let him who is holy continue to be holy.

It will be as on television when the action suddenly freezes, and everyone is fixed into what he was doing at that moment.

When God's patience finally runs out, His judgment will be awesome in its severity. "Our God is a consuming fire" (Hebrews 12:29).

In this day Christ is our ark of safety. We are living now in a time similar to Noah's. God again grieves over the world's sins; He understands its suicidal consequences, and in His longsuffering and grace He does the same three things:

He waits.

He warns.

He makes a way of escape.

"Put a door in the side of the ark," God had told Noah (Genesis 6:16). There was only one way in—but it was clearly there and available to all.

"I am the door," says Jesus to us today. "By me if any man enter in, he shall be saved" (John 10:9 KJV).

The people in Noah's day weren't saved by admiring the ark or by commending Noah for the good job he was doing, or even by helping him build it or by giving to the project! They were saved only by *going in.*

Jesus doesn't say that we today will be saved by living a good life or by admiring Jesus or by working in a church and being religious; we're saved only by *going in the door.* "I am the way," He says. There is only one door, one way. "No one comes to the Father except through me" (John 14:6).

A dear friend of ours in his twenties recently suffered a terrible financial storm. He was sharp and full of energy and overly-optimistic, and he started an ambitious business project that totally crashed. Our friend watched one asset and holding after another disappear.

What did he do? He saw that he'd been trying to get ahead in his own energies, that he'd been living "in the flesh," outside of the parameters of God's blessing. And he saw that there was no hope for his life outside of Him. God let this terrible storm come to bring him to the end of himself. And when our dear friend saw that Jesus Christ was God's ark of safety, he went in.

Whatever this young man's future finances, he has solved the greater problem of his sin and his personal accountability to God. Wonderful! Praise the Lord!

In Him you, too, are protected from all the waters of judgment, from all the destructive judgment of sin. God has shut the door. In Christ you're absolutely safe.

The Hebrew Cities of Refuge: A Second Old Testament Picture

Centuries after the flood God chose a special people, the Jews, and placed them in their "promised land." These Israelites had a different status with God than Noah's contemporaries. Israelites were in the family of God; they were His people. As far as their standing with God was concerned, they weren't "out," they were "in."

But suppose one day one of these Hebrews was out in a field chopping wood with his friend. He's innocently chopping away when suddenly his axe-head loosens from its handle and flies through the air and comes squarely down in his friend's head, hideously cleaving his skull. The man drops, instantly dead.

Worse yet, here comes the man's brother, pounding across the field in revenge, knife in hand and fury on his face.

That Israelite may be safe in God's family as far as eternity's concerned, but on earth he's got a huge problem.

Our consistent God, ever the God of love and mercy, anticipated the danger of unwarranted individual attacks and provided special refuge-cities before the Israelites ever entered their land.

Six cities, equally spaced over the land and with broad, well-kept roads leading to them, were provided for the people. But not just anybody could go in.

Confession opened the door. Says Joshua 20:3, 4,

> Anyone who kills a person accidentally and unintentionally may flee there and find protection from the avenger of blood.
>
> When he flees to one of these cities, he is to stand at the entrance of the city gate and state his case before the elders of that city.

Out of breath, with avengers not far behind, here comes somebody pounding up to the city gate and crying, "Quick! Let me in!"

"Why?" asks the watchman. "What have you done?"

It's essential that he declare the fact: "I killed a man! But I didn't mean to do it!"

When he has "stated his case," according to Joshua 20:4, the gate swings open. Confession is required.

The Difference between the Flood Dilemma and the Manslayer Dilemma

At this point we want to make sure you see the enormous difference between the man pursued by his friend's brother and the man of Noah's day caught in rising floodwaters. These two Old Testament scenes are pictures of two entirely different situations before God.

Noah's contemporaries were shut out of the parameter of the family of faith, sinners far from God, deliberately corrupt and facing His final judgment. Our God of mercy, even then, was offering them an ark as a last-minute escape. That ark was a picture of the Lord Jesus Christ and the salvation that He offers every sinner condemned to hell.

Joshua's contemporaries were *in* the family of Israel; they were God's chosen people, part of His own, and facing death *not as God's final judgment but as the result of a life situation.* Our God of mercy also had a provision for them: to flee to the nearest city of refuge. That city also was a picture of the Lord Jesus Christ and the continuing refuge that He always is for those who are already *in Him.*

When you were first saved, you fled into Christ for your eternal salvation. That was like Christ the ark. Now, as long as you live, and in the midst of every threatening situation, you must continue to flee into Him—as into Christ the city of refuge.

Do you see the difference? As far as your "standing in Christ," you are *in the ark.* You are in Him. This is your eternal position. But practically, concerning your "state" from day to day and as often as you need to, flee *to the city!* Flee anew to Christ.

There's a vast difference between your permanent "standing" in Christ and your temporary "state." Don't get them confused! Believers must never think that when they fall into sin and mess up their "state," that their "standing" is in jeopardy. It is as secure as the promises of God.

There is one similarity: Both situations require confession. When you accepted Christ you said, "I'm helpless on my own; I need you, Jesus." Thereafter you must keep saying, "I'm still helpless on my own, Lord; *I have You but I need You.*" Both are true.

"Just as you received Christ Jesus as Lord, continue to live in him" (Colossians 2:6). You came humbly, confessing your need with words. Flee back "into Him" continually, still confessing your need with words.

Oh, the times in our life when the two of us have been absolutely "up against it," and then we fled to Christ again! What a refuge He is, what a comfort!

Jesus, Lover of my soul,
Let me to Thy bosom fly,
While the nearer billows roll,
While the tempest still is high.
Hide me! Oh, my Saviour, hide
Till the storm of life is past;
Safe into the haven guide—
Oh, receive my soul at last.

Acceptance, provision, and security were all obligatory. Says Joshua 20:4, "[The elders] are to admit him into their city." They had no choice; the law required it!

And Jesus Christ receives you, His child, over and over and over. "Come to me," He says in Matthew 11:28, "and I will give you rest." "Cast all your anxiety on him because he cares for you" (1 Peter 5:7).

The elders were required not only to take the refugee into their city but also to "give him a place to live with them" (Joshua 20:4). Once he got in, they had to support him! He ran to that city of refuge in need, having left all behind. From then on, all his needs would be met.

It's true continually—as we sing,

Nothing in my hands I bring,
Simply to Thy cross I cling.

Matthew 6:33 says, "Seek first his kingdom [seek your City of Refuge, Christ Jesus!] . . . and all these things will be given to you as well." The supply of your material needs is one of the sure promises of God for every one who is "in Christ."

Complete security was obligatory as well.

> If the avenger of blood pursues him, [the elders] must not surrender the one accused, because he killed his neighbor unintentionally and without malice aforethought (Joshua 20:5).

And when Satan, the "avenger of blood," the "accuser of the brothers," comes pounding down the road after you, God says, "You can't touch my child. He is under My personal protection, in a place I Myself have provided: He is *in Christ!*"

Christian, you are forever safe and secure *in Him.* Nothing is more important, as Paul says in Philippians 3:8, 9, than for you to "gain Christ and be found in Him"!

Every time Satan accuses and threatens you, and you discover yourself "out there" in a dangerous environment with feelings of fear and insecurity and vulnerability, flee to Christ again—back to His Word, back to prayer, back to close fellowship with the brothers and sisters, back to humble obedience in every way you can see. This is to be your permanent lifestyle as a Christian here on earth.

And all manslayers were welcome.

In 1886 the United States erected its "Freedom Lady," one of the most colossal sculptures in the history of the world, a gift from the nation of France. She's the Statue of Liberty, and she stands at old Fort Wood on Bedloe's Island in the New York harbor, the very portal of the New World. She has greeted millions of both the oppressed and the adventurous, seeking a fresh start in America. The broken shackles of tyranny lying at her feet have spoken for themselves to generations fleeing tyranny. The torch in her right hand lights the way for newcomers from everywhere to freedom and liberty.

And to all the world she says,

> Give me your tired, your poor,
> Your huddled masses yearning to breathe free,
> The wretched refuse of your teeming shore:
> Send these, the homeless, tempest tossed, to me!
> I lift my lamp beside the golden door.

To be "in America"—that's the dream of millions around the world.

To be "in Christ"—that's the most privileged place of all.

So think about it: From God's floods of judgment upon all the sins of humankind, be sure you've found your "standing" in His ark of safety, the Lord Jesus Christ.

And from Satan's threats and accusations against all the people of God, "in the land" and yet vulnerable in their earthly state, be sure you learn to keep fleeing quickly into God's city of refuge, that same wonderful Lord Jesus Christ.

Understand it, and tell it to Him: *Lord, You are my hiding place.*

Getting Into Christ

The only way sinful people can be saved from the judgment of God is by fleeing into Christ for eternal salvation. The ark of Noah is a good picture of this. But even after salvation, these redeemed men and women must continue to flee into Christ in the midst of every threatening situation--into Jesus, their city of refuge.

Read Colossians 2:6-7

1. How did the Colossians "receive Christ Jesus as Lord" (see vv. 1:21-23)? How did their life in Christ begin?
2. How were the Colossians to continue their life in Christ?
3. How are these two things in questions 1 and 2 related? How are they different?
4. What pictures come to mind when you think of something firmly "rooted" in the ground?

What do you think of when you picture a solid structure? Does your own faith share any of the characteristics of the pictures you just described?

5. How does verse 7 remind you of Romans 7:25?

Read Acts 4:23-31

1. It would no doubt have been easy for Peter and John to slip into "the flesh" during their ordeal described in Acts 4. Why? How do you think they avoided it?
2. Peter and John and the rest of the believers knew they were "up against it." Where did they flee for refuge (vv. 29-30)?
3. What happened when these men and women requested God's help (v. 31)? Why do you think Luke tells us this story?
4. The flesh shows itself in many ways. What are the different ways in which the people mentioned in verses 27-28 demonstrated they were living in the flesh?
5. What difficult circumstances confront you this week? How can the experiences of the early disciples instruct and encourage you?

If you are using this study guide in a group setting, discuss together your answers to the last question and close by praying for each other.

A while back we went on a wonderful cruise on the Mediterranean. Some of us were short, some were tall, some had dark hair, some had no hair at all. We were all different; we were each unique. But we were all on the ship. The point was not what we were like; the point was that we were aboard ship together—for better or for worse. But some had a gift for storytelling, and others could sing or play the piano, and we had a great time.

The Holy Spirit selects unique people and puts them together in Christ. Look around you—and realize that He didn't make any mistakes. You are one in Christ—together.

~ 11 ~

Unified Yet Distinct

Suppose you have a piano, and somebody completely dismantles it. All the screws are taken out, all the strings, all the hammers, all the keys—the whole thing gets piled up into a heap of wood and strings and metal. You can't then say about it, "There's a piano." It has to be in one piece to be a piano.

The church is not an aggregation of strings and metal or anything else. The church is a body of believers "sanctified in Christ Jesus" (1 Corinthians 1:2). When the Spirit so fashions us that we fit together in our particular place, then we're the church, we're "all one in Christ Jesus" (Galatians 3:28). God means for all of us who are in Christ to fit together to make beautiful music.

What makes us fit together? Gifts from the Spirit! The twelfth chapter of 1 Corinthians is helpful here:

> Now about spiritual gifts, brothers, I do not want you to be ignorant. You know that when you

> were pagans, somehow or other you were influenced and led astray to [mute] idols. Therefore I tell you that no one who is speaking by the Spirit of God says, "Jesus be cursed," and no one can say, "Jesus is Lord," except by the Holy Spirit.
>
> There are different kinds of gifts, but the same Spirit. There are different kinds of service, but the same Lord. There are different kinds of working, but the same God works all of them in all men.
>
> Now to each one the manifestation of the Spirit is given for the common good. To one there is given through the Spirit the message of wisdom, to another the message of knowledge by means of the same Spirit, to another faith by the same Spirit, to another gifts of healing by that one Spirit, to another miraculous powers, to another prophecy, to another distinguishing between spirits, to another speaking in different kinds of tongues, and to still another the interpretation of tongues. All these are the work of one and the same Spirit, and He gives them to each one, just as he determines.
>
> The body is a unit, though it is made up of many parts; and though all its parts are many, they form one body. So it is with Christ (1 Corinthians 12:1-12).

Some translations put the word *gifts* in italics. That means it was not in the original, but the translators included it to give the best rendering. *The Living Bible* words it helpfully when it says that God gives to each of us "special abilities."

The first step into Christ, Paul says here, is to call Jesus "Lord." It takes all the force of heaven to call Him "Lord," because it means we turn our backs on all the idolatry of our past lives. We've made a U-turn; we face a new direction.

"In Christ": a new position. "In Christ": a new direction. It's a totally new life, the beginning of a glorious forever.

How Do You Live in Unity?

God's Word says we are one, and that's a fact. (Ephesians 4:4: "There is one body.") But it also often says, "Then live like it!" (Ephesians 4:3: "Make every effort to keep the unity.")

How can we live out our oneness in Christ? Let us suggest four ways from 1 Corinthians 12.

Accept your place in the body of Christ. You're gifted to be you, and nobody else can fulfill your particular spot. You read in verses 4 and 5, "There are different kinds of gifts, but the same Spirit. There are different kinds of service [or ministries], but the same Lord."

How can we describe it? Someone has said the Holy Spirit is like electricity. You could paraphrase these verses, "There are different kinds of appliances—refrigerators, irons, vacuum cleaners, toasters—but the same electrical power."

There are basically four passages in the Bible that list the gifts of the Spirit:

1. 1 Corinthians 12:8-11;
2. 1 Corinthians 12:28-30;
3. Romans 12:6-8; and
4. Ephesians 4:11.

There's also a reference to specific gifts in 1 Peter 4:8-11. Notice that the gifts are for ministry, for helping fellow Christians. The gifts are for results! God wants to use you. He places you into the body of Christ to serve the other members of the body. And as the human body has many parts or members, so all the members function to make a marvelous whole, or, as 1 Corinthians 12:7 says, "for the common good," or "for the common advantage."

Verse 11: "All these [gifts] are the work of one and the same Spirit, and he gives them to each one, just as he determines." It's up to His sovereign prerogative. You can no more choose your gift than you choose the color of your eyes!

Perform your task. Function within the body of Christ. Don't rebel at your place there. Look at verses 15 and 16:

> If the foot should say, "Because I am not a hand, I do not belong to the body," it would not for that reason cease to be a part of the body. And if the ear should say, "Because I am not an eye, I do not belong to the body," it would not for that reason cease to be part of the body.

A feeling of inferiority is a sin against God's wisdom and His plan. Never be caught saying, "I don't amount to anything" or "I'm not important. Why should I be part of a church?" That's a sin against the Holy Spirit. If you're "in Christ," His Spirit has equipped you with everything you need to take your place there.

If your foot would say, "I'm so clumsy; I can't write like the hand; I quit!" you'd be in trouble, wouldn't you? If your ear should say, "I'm not delicate like the eye; I'm through!" that would be a tragedy, wouldn't it?

Don't ever compare yourself disparagingly with other Christians. God never runs out of ideas; He never stamps us out like cookies on a cookie sheet. You're not like others because God designed you to be uniquely you. And He likes what He made. You can't say, "I quit!" and pull away from the body. That's amputation; that's mutilating Christ. You can't say, "I attend church just to slip in and slip out. I don't want to get too involved." Then you're like a paralyzed hand or a withered arm—part of the body but tragically not functioning. God has created you with gifts to minister for the good of the body, for the advantage of everyone else.

To refuse to function, to refuse fellowship with others, to refuse to love, is one of the great sins of the church.

"Well, I just don't feel comfortable in that kind of company," someone may say. Who said you have to feel comfortable? A little pain is inevitable in any relationship. As you get more accustomed to being involved, it will probably get easier.

Or what if you say, "But I don't get anything out of it"? That really has nothing to do with it. We're all there in the body to function: to give, to be, to fit, to belong. The Holy Spirit has equipped you to give, and to reject that is to say no to Him. As members of Christ's body we must all both give and receive—regularly, patiently, constantly.

And allow others to function. Look at verse 18 and following:

> But in fact God has arranged the parts of the body, every one of them, just as he wanted them to be. If they were all one part, where would the body be? As it is, there are many parts, but one body.
>
> The eye cannot say to the hand, "I don't need you!" And the head cannot say to the feet, "I don't need you!"

Just as you mustn't sin through an inferiority complex (verse 15, author's paraphrase, "you don't need me"), so you mustn't sin through a superiority complex (verse 21, "I don't need you!") You and I need everyone in the body, because verse 18 says God has arranged the parts. Therefore we must be willing to accept our limitations so that others can perform their ministry to us!

You are something, but you're not everything! That's hard for some pastors to admit. The congregation really baits them to try to be everything, and they go pell-mell, this direction and that, trying to perform duties for which they aren't gifted. In the meanwhile there's someone sitting right in the congregation, gifted to do just those things.

A management expert once helped us when he said, "Anything that someone else can do 80 percent as well as you, let him do it. Give yourself to those things which only you can do."

Be what you are, but don't take the privilege of functioning away from a brother or sister. Do you pray easily? Learn to listen to a stumbler pray. Do you consider yourself sharp? Esteem others better. The church is a place where we must learn to be mutually dependent.

A group of Christians we know recently divided up in twos. One in each pair was blindfolded while the other was to lead him by the hand, anywhere. The blindfolded one simply had to trust in the goodwill of his leader. One of the men said about his experience, "The first few steps were agony. But when I finally got to the place where I implicitly trusted him, it was one of the greatest lessons I've ever learned."

To do nothing—that's the sin of waste. To try to do everything—that's the sin of pride.

Naturally, we want to be independent. But supernaturally, God can teach us to depend on each other in Him.

Can you think of a weaker member of the body of Christ? Encourage the lesser one to function with honor. Verses 22, 23: "On the contrary, those parts of the body that seem to be weaker are indispensable, and the parts that we think are less honorable we treat with special honor."

As a matter of fact, God usually gives a local congregation one or several members who are mentally or physically or socially deficient. We believe He plants them there to test us and to show the world that we really do love all the body!

Make fellowship happen. Allow others to function, yes; but more. Aggressively help them to do it. Move in, find out about each other, rejoice together, suffer together, plan together, pray together. Act out in practical "body life" what God has already proclaimed to be true. Verses 25-27:

> . . . there should be no division in the body, but . . . its parts should have equal concern for each other. If one part suffers, every part suffers with it; if one part is honored, every part rejoices with it.
>
> Now you are the body of Christ, and each one of you is part of it.

Let us give two illustrations from the story of Paul's conversion. In Acts 9 Saul was looking for Christians to harass or even to kill. Nobody was exempt. He was on his way to Damascus for this very purpose when Jesus Christ confronted him in a blinding light, and he fell to the ground.

And Jesus said an astonishing thing: "Saul, Saul, why do you persecute *me?*"

Saul thought he'd been persecuting Christians! But no, when he persecuted those who were in Christ, he was persecuting Christ Himself.

Christ has so identified with us, and so baptized us into Himself, that to speak roughly about a Christian brother is to speak roughly about Christ. To ignore a brother in Christ is to ignore Christ Himself. To touch another Christian's reputation is to touch the reputation of Christ. To make fun of a believer is to make fun of Jesus. "Now you are the body of Christ, and each one of you is part of it."

Here's the second point of this story of Paul's conversion. When Paul was a brand new convert, what was the first step he had to take? Jesus didn't stand there on the Damascus road and spell out His orders directly to Paul, the new convert. He said, "There's a man in the city whose name is Ananias. He's just an ordinary disciple. He's 'number four' on the list of those you were going to kill. I want you to get your orders from him, a brother in my family. He'll tell you what to do."

Christ did not personally give Paul directions. Even though he was a "big fish" on the line, Paul's first lesson was to learn to submit to another member of the body.

You have two choices. You can have a pre-Damascus Road mentality, judging, criticizing, actually persecuting the Lord Jesus. Or you can submit yourself to your brothers and sisters in Christ and humbly take your orders from them—from Him!

What's the difference between these two frames of mind? Repentance—a fresh meeting with Jesus, a deliberate humbling of yourself. It's saying, "Lord, what would you have me do?"

When Paul did this, the magnificent result was peace in the church, and many were added to the fellowship.

Christian, do you persecute your fellow believers? Faultfinding isn't hard; any fool can do that. But building up a brother is a godly ministry. And John 17:21, 23 says that that kind of activity is what will bring the world to believe.

In a mysterious, even mystical way, we must see Christ in our corporate body of brothers and sisters. Then you can exclaim, *"Oh, Church, you are my hiding place"*—and it will indeed become a refuge.

Getting Into Christ

All believers are one in Christ, but that doesn't mean they're all the same. You have a unique place in the body and an assigned task that only you can fulfill. It's up to each one of us to discover our role, to do what only we are gifted to do, and then help others in the body to do the same.

Read Romans 12:4-8

1. Verses 4-5 say the church is like a body in four ways: (a) There is only one body; (b) This one body is made up of several individual parts; (c) Each part has a unique and indispensable function; (d) Each part belongs to every other part. Which of these truths is hardest for you to grasp? Which is hardest for you to put into practice?
2. How would you present the four truths outlined in question 1 to a hermit who tells you it's best for Christians to seek and serve God in solitude?
3. Verse 6 says different people have different gifts. How can this very fact sometimes cause friction in the church? What ways can you think of to minimize the possibility?
4. It's quite possible you don't see your own gift mentioned in this list; in fact, there probably is no exhaustive list of gifts in Scripture. One way to define spiritual gifts is, "any ability or special endowment that helps the church to grow and mature." With this definition in mind, what "gifts" do you think you have?

Read Acts 6:1-7

1. How is this story an illustration of Romans 12:4-8?
2. How did those first seven deacons discover their gifts?
3. How did the deacons' use of their gifts benefit the church? What was the result (v. 7)?
4. What do you think would have happened to the church if these men had refused to do what they were gifted for?

5. Verse 1 makes it clear that dissension existed in the early church. How did their understanding of the church as a body help them work through their problems? How could it help yours?

If you are using this study guide in a group setting, discuss together how you can use your gifts to help your church grow. Close in prayer, asking God's help in this.

For Paul the Christian life is not merely a memory of a God-man who lived once and is gone. It is not an imitation of a good life. It is not a momentary ecstatic experience.

The whole of life, from its fundamental being to its discrete actions, is surrounded by the reality of Christ. The pilgrim journey is not a burdensome trudge up a lonely road; it is a way that cuts through and is always within the environment of Jesus Christ Himself. Life begins, proceeds, and ends in Christ.

Lewis B. Smedes,
<u>All Things Made New</u>

12

Abiding in Christ

If you're eternally in Christ, why would you have to be told to "abide" there?

Because, terrible but true, there can be a great difference between where God has placed us and how we act about it. It's as if a bride was standing at the altar being married to a really wonderful man, and as soon as the ceremony was over, she turned, yawned, and took a nap on the platform.

God's message to you is loud and clear: Understand your position in Christ and live it to the hilt.

God brought the Israelites out of Egypt by a miracle, but subsequently they wandered around for forty years in the desert. Why? Because having been brought out of, they weren't too sure they wanted to enter into. Christians, too, can be genuinely saved (from God's wrath and eternal punishment) and yet not live in Christ in their day-by-day experience. What a tragedy!

Jesus spelled out our need to consciously, obediently come into Him in John 15. Let's look at it:

> I am the true vine, and My Father is the vinedresser. Every branch in Me that does not bear fruit, He takes away; and every branch that bears fruit, He prunes it, that it may bear more fruit. You are already clean because of the word which I have spoken to you. Abide in Me, and I in you. As the branch cannot bear fruit of itself, unless it abides in the vine, so neither can you, unless you abide in Me.
>
> I am the vine, you are the branches; he who abides in Me, and I in him, he bears much fruit; for apart from Me you can do nothing. If anyone does not abide in Me, he is thrown away as a branch, and dries up; and they gather them, and cast them into the fire, and they are burned. If you abide in Me, and My words abide in you, ask whatever you wish, and it shall be done for you. By this is My Father glorified, that you bear much fruit, and so prove to be My disciples.
>
> Just as the Father has loved Me, I have also loved you; abide in My love. If you keep My commandments, you will abide in My love; just as I have kept My Father's commandments, and abide in His love. These things I have spoken to you, that My joy may be in you, and that your joy may be made full (John 15:1-11 NAS).

Verse 16:

> You did not choose Me, but I chose you, and appointed you, that you should go and bear fruit, and that your fruit should remain, that whatever you ask of the Father in My Name, He may give to you.

Jesus often talked of things at hand; he was keenly aware of life around Him. If He walked on earth today His illustrations might come from the stock market, or a hot car, or smog—and through them he would broaden our minds with deep, rich truths, expanding us beyond anything we've experienced.

If you're seeking a spiritually rich life, you want something grander for the future than you've ever known. That's the hunger Christ put in your heart. Don't deny it; don't quench it.

Don't say, as many are apt to, "Well, this is just too lofty for me. I'm not this type of person." None of us is, in ourselves! We're all sinners: "All we like sheep have gone astray." Somehow we seem to get comfort from the fact that others are just as bad as we are. We like to think, "I'm not too good, I'm not too bad. I kind of fit."

But in that attitude you miss the very blessing, the very glory of life. You live like that and you'll settle for a half-life, an incomplete life. Venture out and say, "I'm going to live with the Lord Jesus continually; I'm going to abide in Him, speaking with Him, praising Him. I'm going to live with God!"

Meister Eckhart said, "There are plenty to follow our Lord halfway, but not the other half. They will give up possessions, friends, and honors, but it touches them too closely to disown themselves."

Disown yourself! "Not I, but Christ" is the whole secret of abiding in Him. "He must become greater," said John the Baptist; "I must become less" (John 3:30). This may be painful for a moment, but the result is worth it!

Here's how Frank Laubach describes his abiding in Christ:

> Worries have faded away like ugly clouds, and my soul rests in the sunshine of perpetual peace. I can lie down anywhere in this universe, bathed around by my own Father's Spirit. The very universe has come to seem so homey! I know only a little more about it than before, but that little is

> all! It is vibrant with the electric ecstasy of God! I know what it means to be "God-intoxicated."[1]

Get it straight: You are either centered in Christ, abiding in Him, or you're centered in man. There is no alternative. Either Christ is the center of your universe and you are adjusting everything to Him, or you yourself have become the center, and you're struggling to make everything orbit around you and for you, and you're miserable! Listen—you were made for God!

Let's pick apart John 15:1-11 and see several truths it's saying to us.

Abide In Christ

How do you abide in Christ? Certainly in your mind, as an act of your will, you decide to abide in Him before you ever understand what you decided. You simply determine to plant yourself "in Christ," to camp day by day on that settled, permanent dwelling spot in which you're going to flourish—sort of like the tree in Psalm 1.

You want to live in vital union with Him because in Him are the perfect conditions for living, like a tree that would never do as well in any other spot. So you "let your roots grow down into Him and draw up nourishment from Him."

Colossians 2:9, 10 (The Living Bible) tells you why He is the best of all possible soils: "In Christ there is all of God. . . so you have everything when you have Christ, and you are filled with God through your union with Christ." The tree planted deep in Him feeds on all of God.

> The pursuit of God . . . must not be casual. [It's] not a part-time, weekend exercise. . . . Abiding requires a kind of staying power. The pursuit is relentless. It hungers and thirsts. It pants as a

1. Frank Laubach, *Letters of a Modern Mystic* (Old Tappan, N.J.: Fleming H. Revell Co.), p. 117.

> deer after the mountain brook. It takes the Kingdom by storm, pressing with violence to get in.
>
> It is a pursuit of passion. Indifference will not do. To abide . . . is to hang on tenaciously. A weak grip will soon slip away. Discipleship with Jesus requires staying power. We sign up for the duration. We do not graduate until heaven.[2]

Some people are spiritual gypsies. They alternate between spiritual spurts and spiritual lethargy. For them there's no calm persistence and rest of heart.

Some just "visit" Christ; they generally like Him, but they don't hang around too much. For some He's only a "shelter in the time of storm."

For others He's an eternal home.

When we probe for ways to abide, of course we must mention church going, prayer, Bible study, and so on. But Christians can have these things in their lives for years and yet never begin to abide in Him. Surely the heart's desire comes first.

Nevertheless, you can't abide in Him without prayer (John 15:7). To abide means to keep the fellowship and the worship lines open. And it certainly means to feed on His Word. It means opening ourselves up to every possible exposure of Him, every possible "means of grace."

"Seek first his kingdom [that is, the kingdom of God] and his righteousness" (Matthew 6:33). The verb "seek" there denotes aggressive action, like a hunter "beating the bushes" for his prey, going after it with all his powers.

George Fox, the founder of Quakerism in the mid-1600s, was a man with a passion to know God and to abide in Him; to know, not merely religion, but God in Christ Himself. He went everywhere querying ministers

---

2. R.C. Sproul, *One Holy Passion* (Nashville, Tenn.: Thomas Nelson, 1987), p. 63.

or priests or laymen, anyone who could possibly tell him how he might really know God.

His relatives said, "What you need, George, is to get married." A priest advised him to smoke tobacco and sing psalms. Another minister got angry and wouldn't even answer because George had stepped in his flower bed! Still another told him that what he really needed was some medicine and a good blood-letting.

For him, the answer wasn't in seminary training. But by abiding in Christ and in His Word, day by day, step by step, George Fox eventually came to know the Lord Himself and came to write this:

> Unless you know God, every day communing with Him, rejoicing in Him, exulting in Him, opening your life in joyful obedience toward Him, and feeling Him speaking to you and guiding you into ever fuller obedience to Him—you aren't fit to be a minister.

Or we could apply this more broadly and say you're not even fit to be a Christian.

In the Vine

When you abide in Christ, you're where the action is. You're caught up in the loftiest, most important levels of life. Jesus Christ is "square one," and anything not related to Him is ultimately meaningless and futile.

Christ is not only the stock, He's the root, the branches—everything. "I am the true vine," He said. Christ and His church are the whole planting of God.

Look again at the words of John 15. Some ten times the word abide or remain appears. You see it three times in verse 4, then in verse 5, and again in 6, 7, 9, and 10. To be a Christian is to be in Christ—and the great need is to stay there, to abide in Him.

Swiss theologian Frédéric Godet says, "Abiding is that continuous act whereby we lay aside all that which we derive from ourselves, to draw from Christ by faith."

A fellow once visited his friend, a music teacher. The visitor said, "Well, what's the good news today?" The teacher went over to a tuning fork, struck it, and said, "That, my friend, is A. It was A all day yesterday. It will be A all day today, tomorrow, next week, and for a thousand years. The soprano upstairs warbles off-key. The tenor next door flats on the high notes. The piano across the hall is often out of tune. But that"—striking the tuning fork again—"that is A. And that's the good news today!"

Christian friend, the truth is that Christ is "A"! When you abide in Him, you are where it's at! Terrible grammar but magnificent truth.

> Change and decay in all around I see;
> O Thou Who changest not, abide with me.

Christ abides with you, and you abide with Him, and the position of both of you is immovable.

Pruning Means Health

Because God is a faithful Gardener, you can be sure that now and then He's going to prune His branches. That's what Jesus says in verse 2: "He cuts off every branch . . . that bears no fruit, while every branch that does bear fruit He prunes [trims clean] so that it will be even more fruitful."

Every branch, sooner or later, is cut by the knife. Pruning cleans up the vine to keep it vital and strong. God trims off anything that will hinder your strength so that you might be fully enabled to produce luscious, beautiful fruit. Through His pruning work, God is training and developing His own.

What does God, the faithful Gardener, trim away from you? Possibly four things.

First, God prunes you of sin. When you first accepted the Lord your concept of sin was superficial, and your trimming could be only superficial and partial. But the more you experience what it is to be "in Christ," the more radical the surgery can be, and the more eager you will be for fully matured fruit in your life.

He will help you cut off the one in order to more fully receive the other. He will help you lose your life to find it. He will help you sell everything to buy the treasure. He will help you to release in order to receive back.

And he will use a very sharp knife.

> To be united with Jesus in His death means for the believer a complete and drastic break with sin. . . . [His life] must reproduce towards sin the implacable hostility which Jesus declared to it by His death.[3]

Second, God prunes you of self-righteousness. The immature Christian has never parted from acts of man-made religion; he simply labels them "Christianity." He wades into the life of the church with his old nature waving like a flag over his head, and his brand new religious life joins his old social life, business life, family life, and all the rest as one more act of the flesh.

Self-help and self-righteousness must go. The impulses of the old nature must be pruned away. Says Andrew Murray,

> There can be no entire abiding in Christ without the giving up of all that is self in religion—without giving it up to the death, and waiting for the breathings of the Holy Spirit as alone able to work in us what is acceptable in God's sight.[4]

---

3. James S. Stewart, *A Man In Christ* (New York and London: Harper and Brothers), pp.187, 188.

4. Andrew Murray, *Abide in Christ* (New York: Grosset and Dunlap), pp.119, 120.

Third, God has the right to prune you of all your lawful occupations and possessions. The fishnets of Peter, James and John, and the household duties of Mary and Martha all served the world's scheme of things until they were turned over to Christ. He says to forsake all and follow Him. In your heart, do that. Then it's up to Him whether He wants to retain these things because He has need of them, or to ask you to relinquish them altogether.

He chose to prune away the fishnets of the men. He chose to retain the household duties of the sisters. It was up to Him. The more your heart has totally surrendered them all, the more complete your abiding will be.

Fourth, God has the right to prune you of your natural talents and abilities. At first that seems silly. When we accept Christ, shouldn't we start exercising our natural gifts for Him?

But everything we have, in ourselves, is still defiled by sin and under the influence of the flesh. We know how religious people can rise to great prominence and then be exposed as "Elmer Gantrys," using their natural abilities for their own corrupt ends.

God has the right to cut away all that we can do in ourselves. We must surrender to let Him do it, if He desires. Then what He leaves *is surrendered to Him*; it's His property, bearing His stamp and revealing His influence, and used only under His total control. Not only your natural talents and abilities, but even your spiritual gifts must be laid humbly on the altar at Jesus' feet.

In this age of narcissism some Christians are pouncing on spiritual gifts in an over-emphasis on self-analyses and test ings and comparisons. Says Adolph Monod, "You must not gloat over your gifts, counting them like treasures, but spend them immediately and remain poor, 'looking unto Jesus.' "

As soon as you begin to get self-satisfied in the possession of spiritual gifts, the "inflow of grace is retarded," as Andrew Murray says, and stagnation threatens.

Stay centered on Christ! Stay humble! Stay amazed at what He's given, and eager to give it back to Him. Let the flow be two-way and full of love.

This is abiding in Christ.

Thomas à Kempis says this in his classic *The Imitation of Christ*:

> Lord, Thou hast put aside my plans, but only that I might open up my eyes to see the depth and the clearness of Thy plan for me.
> Thou hast not spared my vanity and my pride; every high thought in me Thou hast struck down, but only that I might find how dear I am to Thee. Finish, then, Thy discipline of me, even though it be by fire; and out of the flames will I praise Thee!

If you've been pruned recently, God is beautifully shaping you to be a fruit-bearer. Your place is simply to "trust and obey," to abide. The only work for a branch is to remain in the vine and draw, and draw, and draw.

A Problem Passage

Christ's pruning of dead wood in John 15:6 is a difficult verse. It says,

> If anyone does not abide in Me, he is thrown away as a branch, and dries up; and they gather them, and cast them into the fire, and they are burned (NAS).

Here's a Christian who once drew strength from Christ, but now he doesn't. He's no longer abiding. If we want to interpret this Scripture correctly, we must interpret it in the light of the great stream of the teaching of the Word of God. And that says, when you're a believer, God keeps you. That truth isn't a thread through Scripture, it's a whole rope! In John 6:37 Jesus says, "Whoever comes to me I will never drive away." We could duplicate that over and over.

So the branch, or the child of God, isn't to be lost. But it can be that he falls away from fruitbearing and usefulness, even though he doesn't fall away from salvation.

A key to this Scripture may be the word-picture that comes out of Ezekiel 15:2-4, which says that the vine has two functions: one, more noble, to bear fruit; the other, less noble, to serve as kindling wood. In John 15:6 the men gather the dead branches and throw them into a fire.

Christian, if you're not abiding, if you're not bearing fruit, God gives you over to less noble usefulness. He says, "All right, if that's all you want to be, so be it. If you simply want to be an accountant, then all you'll be is an accountant; that's it. Or you'll be just a housewife; that's all. Or if you're determined just to be a student, then study, study, study. That's all you'll be! Or if you're going to be part of an office crew, then you'll just be part of an office crew. That's it!"

People will use you. There's nothing wrong with that—you won't be a "zero," but neither will you be bearing fruit unto God for eternity and glory for Him. There will be nothing supernatural, nothing great, only momentary and lesser activities going on in your life.

In 1 Corinthians 3:15 Paul writes of the same thing: "If [a man's work] is burned up, he will suffer loss; he himself will be saved, but only as one escaping through the flames."

Jesus gives yet another illustration of greater and lesser usefulness in the Sermon on the Mount. "You are the salt of the earth," He says. "But if the salt loses its saltiness, how can it be made salty again? It's no longer good for its highest intended use—salt for the table—but only to keep the ice off the ground in cold weather, to be thrown out and trampled down by men" (authors' paraphrase). That's certainly a far lesser use.

The glorious alternative is for you to abide in Him and bear eternal fruit to God, fruit like love, joy, peace, patience, kindness, goodness, faithfulness, gentleness and self-control (Galatians 5:22, 23). It's Christ-likeness. His characteristics become your characteristics. His life is displayed in your life. Remember, you don't make the fruit, you only bear it.

And you're never static. John 15 talks about "fruit," "more fruit," "much fruit," and "fruit that will last." You, as a believer, are in the process of becoming and becoming and becoming.

Older Christians, you must keep on becoming! Don't get locked into yesterday. You're either becoming or you're degenerating. No one is static. "By their fruits you shall know them," says Jesus. Fruit is the outward evidence of inner life.

Of course it's hard to have the patience to develop this quality of life. We want success quickly. On television every mystery is solved in a few minutes; every laundry problem is taken care of in twenty-nine seconds. But abiding in Christ takes time.

Abiding is not a self-improvement scheme. If you seek God just to become a better Christian, you've missed the whole point. This isn't for you, it's for Him. This is to dwell in Him, to settle down in Him, to make Him your most familiar surroundings—to abide in Him (verses 4 and 5), to abide in His love (verses 9 and 10), to give Him glory and pleasure.

And this is not a one-time commitment, it's a daily one. It calls you from all double-mindedness to single-mindedness.

Now let us tell you something wonderful. God began a process at your new birth which is irreversible. Like it or not, kick and scream if you will, if you're a true believer, "he who began a good work in you will carry it on to completion until the day of Christ Jesus" (Philippians 1:6).

If you saw a tadpole when he's half frog, you wouldn't say he's a hypocrite, you'd say he's in the process of becoming a frog. And so with you and us. We're on our way from earthly to heavenly!

Kids progress, don't they?—they metamorphose. They're one thing when they're two years old and another when they're eight or fifteen or twenty-two.

My friend, be sure of this: Just as genes dictate that a tadpole will someday be a frog, and that a baby will grow to be an adult, so God dictates that you will someday be like Christ. You're in Christ, and His meter is running.

In the fall, flocks of geese and ducks head south. They may land on a pond and feed a while, but soon, however pleasant that surrounding may be, instinct calls them out into the blue and down to the south to their home.

The home of every Christian is already "in Christ." But in the heart of every one of us, placed there by God, is the instinct to *go there* and to settle down and remain there in His continual presence and love.

Praise God for our homing instinct! He stirs it up; He moves it. Your heart will always be restless until it rests in Him. He has made you for Himself.

A few years ago the "Ray" half of us resigned from the church where he'd been pastor for twenty years, hearing God's call to take a year for study and to seek His face afresh.

His first Sunday in a different church was miserable. It felt so strange to sit in a pew. He felt lost, cut off, orphaned, depressed. He was critical of the pastor up front. He kept thinking, I could do it better!

Finally in his agony he began to write on the margin of the church bulletin. "Ray Ortlund," he wrote, "is your identity only in being in the pulpit, or is your identity in Christ?"

He thought and prayed about that for a while. Then he wrote further on that church bulletin, "Lord Jesus Christ, I want my identity to be only in You. If I never ever preach again, but only worship and praise You as long as I live, I promise to be absolutely content."

It was a turning point in his life. God had done some more pruning. He had gotten rid of some ego; it was a crisis that was the beginning of a process.

Since then Ray has been preaching over four hundred times a year, in many places, and God is helping him not to think of himself as "in a pulpit" but "in Christ." Abiding there, he bears fruit, offering to God "a sacrifice of praise—the fruit of lips that confess his name" (Hebrews 13:15).

"In Christ." We are in Him, and we're learning more to abide there. We're beginning to say more consistently, "Oh Lord Jesus Christ, *You are our hiding place*!"

How about you?

Write to us. We'd love to hear how you're doing!

Warmly in Christ,

Ray and Anne Ortlund
32 Whitewater Drive
Corona del Mar, CA 92625
U.S.A.

Getting Into Christ

There's only one road to full maturity in Christ, and that's by abiding in Him. What does that mean? It means that we spend time in the Scriptures. It means that we spend time in prayer. It means that the Great Gardener, Jesus, will cut us and prune us to make us more fruitful. And it means that we dwell in Him, settle down in Him, and blossom there.

Read John 15:1-12

1. Jesus calls Himself the "true" vine. Are there other vines that are not "true"? Describe them.
2. Compare John 15:1-2 with Hebrews 12:5-11. What do they have in common? What is your emotional response to their teaching? What response do you think their authors were hoping for in their readers?
3. Have you ever tried to bear fruit apart from Christ? Did people notice right away? How did it end up?
4. How do we prove we are Jesus' disciples (v. 8)? What does it accomplish?
5. What personal tests can you use to judge whether you are abiding in Christ?

Read Acts 11:19-30

1. Do you think the believers described in this passage were abiding in Christ? Why?
2. Verse 23 says that Barnabas saw "evidence of the grace of God" among new believers in Antioch. What do you guess this "evidence" might have been? Do you see any similar evidence in your own life?
3. Which verses in this passage illustrate Jesus' words in John 15:8?
4. Which verses in this passage illustrate Jesus' words in John 15:12?
5. If abiding in Christ provides so many benefits, why do many of us find it so hard to do? What practical steps can we take to encourage each other to abide in him, as did the persecuted church described in this passage?

If you are using this study guide in a group setting, close the study by discussing the last question together. Take hands around your circle and pray for each other, praying for the person on your right. Then take five minutes for everyone to give thanks to God for the blessings you enjoy in Christ.

Paul began his letter to the Philippian believers like this: "To all the saints in Christ Jesus at Philippi" (Philippians 1:1).

Think about that. As I broadcast this message to you I am "at" Los Angeles, but thank God, I am also "in" Christ. You listen where you are—"at" Miami, Florida, or "at" Saskatchewan, Canada, or "at" Capetown, South Africa, or "at" Manila, Philippines, or "at" Quito, Ecuador. You are "at" a location, but if you're a believer, you're also "in" Christ. Your geographical location is temporary, but your spiritual location in Christ is permanent.

And I promise you, if you're most conscious of your geographical location—even as a Christian, you're upset and full of fears. But if you're most conscious of your spiritual location in Christ—if you're practicing His presence, aware of His love and care, depending on His wisdom and guidance—my friend, you're full of peace and joy.

Selection from the April 27, 1987
"Haven of Rest" Broadcast,
Dr. Ray Ortlund

Appendix

"In Christ"—As Seen in Paul's Letters to the Churches

"Those three short words, 'In Christ Jesus,' are without doubt the most important ever written, even by an inspired pen, to express the mutual relationship of the believer and Christ."[1]

Being in Christ means—

He surrounds you (Colossians 3:4);

He separates you from everything that's hostile or dangerous (1 John 5:18, 19);

He supplies everything you need (Philippians 4:19).

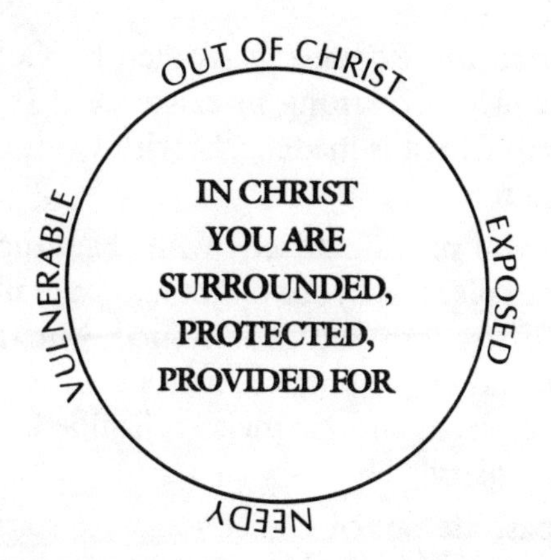

1. A. T. Pierson, *In Christ Jesus* (Chicago: Moody Press, 1974), p.9.

Christ is the living space, the breathing air, the atmosphere of your life!

Go with us through the letters of Paul to the churches, to see that God wants you to be absorbed with the awareness of where you are: in Christ. He says it over and over, from every possible angle.

Romans: In Christ Justified

Here Paul says that in Christ you are made totally righteous in His very own righteousness:

Romans says:

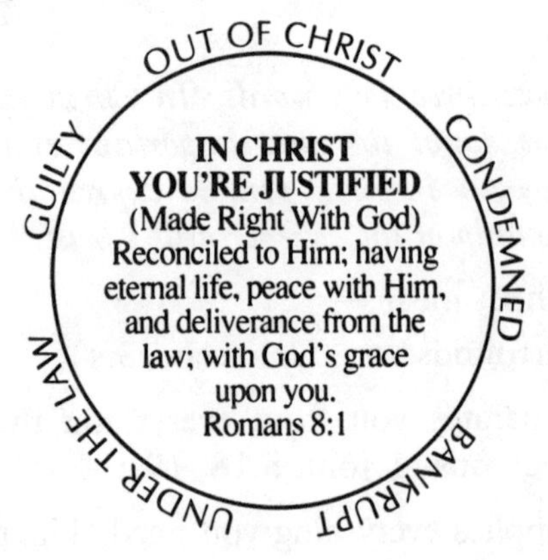

Paul's letter to the Romans was called by Coleridge "the profoundest piece of writing in existence." It teaches that the believer in Christ is made right with God; he is justified in God's sight.

Suppose you're threatened with bankruptcy, and a wealthy friend discovers your plight and pays all your debts. In your own strength you'd be ruined, but through your friend's care and by his financial actions on your behalf you are totally cleared and financially justified. You'll sing! You'll have a party!

In your past life out of Christ you were spiritually bankrupt. But Jesus not only paid your debt of sin and made you clean and clear before Him, but He applied to your account all His own righteousness. He made you rich in His own goodness!

> This righteousness from God comes through faith in Jesus Christ to all who believe. There is no difference, for all have sinned and fall short of the glory of God, and are justified freely by his grace through the redemption that came by Christ Jesus. . . .
>
> Therefore, since we have been justified through faith, we have peace with God through our Lord Jesus Christ. . . .
>
> Therefore, there is now no condemnation for those who are in Christ Jesus (Romans 3:22-24, 5:1, 8:1).

1 and 2 Corinthians: In Christ Sanctified

"To the church of God in Corinth, to those sanctified in Christ Jesus and called to be holy . . . " (1 Corinthians 1:2). Paul starts his first letter to the Corinthians with his direction set. He's writing about sanctification—being separated from the world, the flesh, and the devil by being in Christ.

Corinthians says:

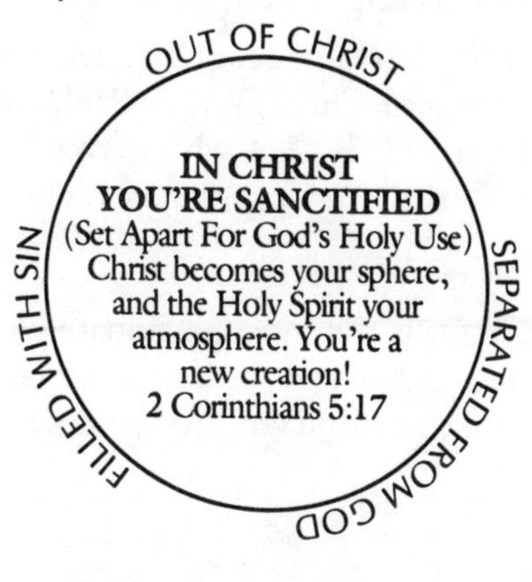

The Greek city of Corinth had become notoriously evil, a hard place for Christians to live. The very term to "Corinthianize" meant to "go to the dogs".

In these letters Paul has a "shopping list"—a list of attitudes and practices that don't belong to those "sanctified in Christ Jesus." In chapter 1, verse 10, he starts with their divisive attitudes: "I appeal to you, brothers, in the name of our Lord Jesus Christ, that all of you agree with one another so that there may be no divisions among you and that you may be perfectly united in mind and thought."

Later he admonishes them about an immoral brother in their number, about lawsuits between them, and other problems.

"He who unites himself with the Lord is one with him in spirit" (6:17). Your union with Christ changes you, says Paul. It should sanctify your personal life and your church life. You're different, you're in Christ.

After some very stormy words the letter ends, "My love to all of you in Christ Jesus. Amen." No matter what their sins, in Christ Paul was still their brother.

But Paul's second letter was even stormier. Here a wounded apostle is letting his hurts show. His pen almost drips with tears that the Corinthians had misunderstood him and were rejecting his ministry.

Certainly the secret to being bonded lovingly to each other is our union in Christ. Writes Paul, struggling to get through to them, "It is God who makes both us and you stand firm in Christ" (2 Corinthians 1:21).

Galatians: In Christ Free

This little letter is the most passionate of all Paul's writings, so strongly did he feel about our not being "entangled again in the yoke of bondage" to the law.

Galatians says:

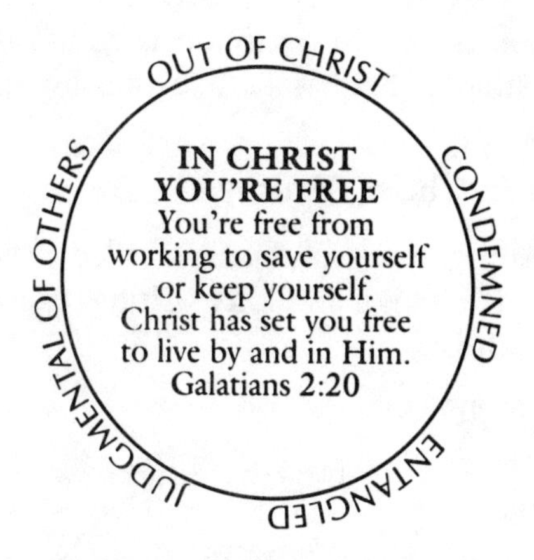

Among the Galatians were those who imposed rules and regulations for the Christian life, thus adding to the gospel. Being "in Christ" was not enough for them! Paul knew about their tactics from his own bitter and embarrassing experiences: "Some false brothers . . . infiltrated our ranks to spy on the freedom we have in Christ Jesus and to make us slaves" (Galatians 2:4). Since they had also made inroads into the Galatian church and had shaken up not a few, Paul wrote, "Are you so foolish? After beginning with the Spirit, are you now trying to attain your goal by human effort?" (3:3).

It's no gospel at all if it's "Christ plus" anything! It's not believing plus keeping the law. The law is only a mirror to show us how dirty we are; it can't wash our faces! The Galatians had been told by these Judaizers to believe in Christ, but also to maintain certain Jewish rites. With strong emotion Paul wrote that grace can't be tinkered with, that it's faith in Christ alone which saves, and faith in Christ alone which helps believers progress along the way.

Your freedom in Christ is more than a comfort; it's a command! "It is for freedom that Christ has set us free. Stand firm, then, and do not let yourselves be burdened again by a yoke of slavery" (5:1). "For in Christ Jesus neither circumcision nor uncircumcision has any value. The only thing that counts is faith expressing itself through love" (5:6).

Ephesians: In Christ Wealthy

Paul's letter to the Ephesians is called "the Alps of the Scriptures." It's a high and lofty writing, expressing all that we have in Christ.

Ephesians says:

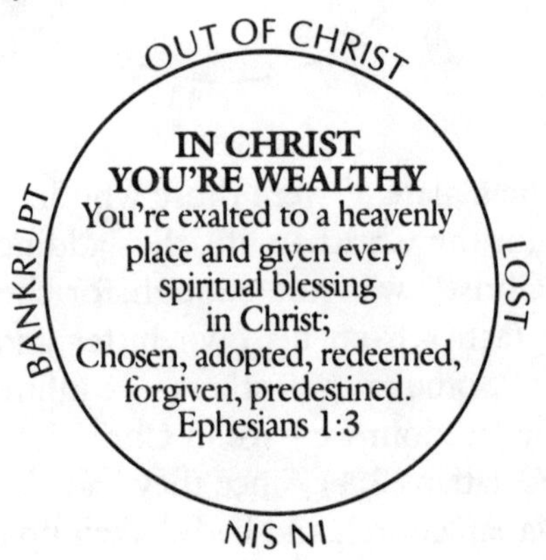

The book of Ephesians pictures you in Christ—fortified, enclosed in His love, housed in His holiness. In chapter 1 alone, the phrase "in Christ" or "in Him" is mentioned eleven times. It starts out saying God "has blessed us in the heavenly realms with every spiritual blessing in Christ" (verse 3). Then the whole letter continues to list our riches in Christ: chosen in Him, verse 4; predestined, verse 5; redeemed and forgiven, verse 7; and so on.

With a broader brush we see that in Christ—

We are made alive and useful, 2:1-10;
We are reconciled with others, 2:11-22;
We share in God's grand purposes, 3:1-13;
We have fullness of knowledge and love, 3:14-21.

In this book Paul is not combating error. He's sharing a vision of the exalted Christ and his overall desires for the church and for you. In the letter to the Ephesians you get the results of Paul's deep maturity.

Philippians: In Christ Rejoicing

"Rejoice in the Lord always," writes Paul; "I will say it again: Rejoice!" (Philippians 4:4).

Philippians says:

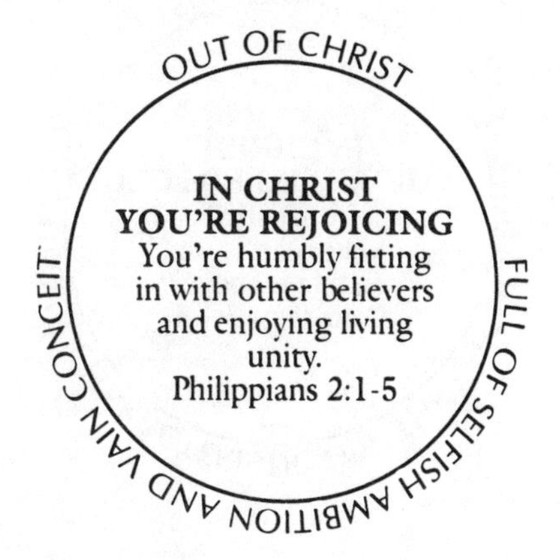

In his letter to the Philippians, Paul says that you're in Christ whatever your circumstances. Paul was in prison, but in Christ, and the letter is full of joy. Link Acts 16:25 and Philippians 4:4 in your Bible, and see that no matter what circumstances you are "in," being in Christ overrides everything.

Notice the loving relationships Paul cultivated (1:1-11) and the opportunities he used to witness to outsiders (1:12-30). See that having the mind of Christ makes us pour out ourselves for others, as did Timothy and Epaphroditus (chapter 2). Reaching, stretching after Christ Jesus (chapter 3) is enough, and in Him even our physical needs will be met (chapter 4).

Colossians: In Christ Filled

How complete are the Colossians! What models they are! "We have heard," writes Paul, "of your *faith* in Christ Jesus and of the *love* you have for all the saints—the faith and love that spring from the *hope* that is stored up for you in heaven . . . " (Colossians 1:4, 5, italics ours).

Colossians says:

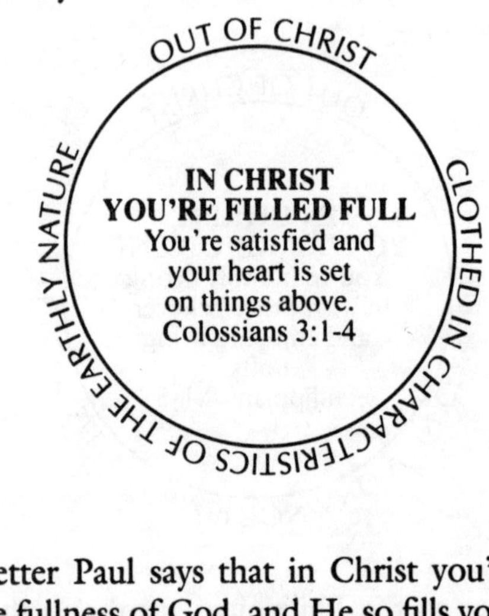

In this letter Paul says that in Christ you're filled full. Christ is the fullness of God, and He so fills you so that you also are full. The whole book gives you the impression of being filled full, pressed down, and running over! The Greek word for "fullness" used in this little letter is so intensely meaningful that it really has no English equivalent.

There is a sense here of total completion in Christ, and, amazingly, that Christ is also made complete when we are in Him! It's not that Christ is *inadequate* without us, but that He is not *satisfied* without us. He is our fullness—and we are His fullness, "the fullness of him [Christ] who fills everything in every way" (Ephesians 1:23); or, as Paul says it here in this letter, "In Christ all the fullness of the Deity lives in bodily form, and you have been given fullness in Christ" (2:9, 10).

1 and 2 Thessalonians: In Christ Ready For His Coming

"Wait for [God's] Son from heaven, whom he raised from the dead," writes Paul to the Thessalonians, "—Jesus, who rescues us from the coming wrath" (1:10).

Thessalonians says:

In 1 and 2 Thessalonians, a future-oriented pair of books, Paul spells out what awaits those who are in Christ:

Rewards (1 Thessalonians 2:19);

Final holiness (1 Thessalonians 3:13);

Reunion with loved ones (1 Thessalonians 4:13-18);

Triumph over death (1 Thessalonians 4:16, 17);

Living forever with Christ (1 Thessalonians 4:17);

The destruction of the "man of sin" (2 Thessalonians 2:8);

The final glory of Jesus Christ (2 Thessalonians 2:14); and many more wonderful things.

The Core of It All

The sweep through Paul's letters to the churches has been fast, but there's no doubt that, with a hundred ramifications, whoever you are, Christian, and wherever you are, you're *in Christ!*

Paul was dominated by both the truth and the experience of it. He was "full of fullness" in Christ. And so must we be! Being in Christ is not an extra, an additive, to the Christian life, it is the core of it all; it is Christianity crystallized. The more you delve into God's Word and immerse yourself in its teaching and implications, the more you will understand and live in the light of being ***in Christ***.[2]

2. The diagrams in this chapter are somewhat similar to those used by A. T. Pierson in his book *In Christ Jesus* (Chicago: Moody Press, 1974).